Crime, Punishment, and Mental Illness

CRITICAL ISSUES IN CRIME AND SOCIETY

Raymond J. Michalowski, Series Editor

Critical Issues in Crime and Society is oriented toward critical analysis of contemporary problems in crime and justice. The series is open to a broad range of topics including specific types of crime, wrongful behavior by economically or politically powerful actors, controversies over justice system practices, and issues related to the intersection of identity, crime, and justice. It is committed to offering thoughtful works that will be accessible to scholars and professional criminologists, general readers, and students.

Tammy L. Anderson, ed., *Neither Villain Nor Victim: Empowerment and Agency among Women Substance Abusers*

Luis A. Fernandez, *Policing Dissent: Social Control and the Anti-Globalization Movement*

Mary Bosworth and Jeanne Flavin, eds., *Race, Gender, and Punishment: From Colonialism to the War on Terror*

Michael J. Lynch, *Big Prisons, Big Dreams: Crime and the Failure of America's Penal System*

Raymond J. Michalowski and Ronald C. Kramer, eds., *State-Corporate Crime: Wrongdoing at the Intersection of Business and Government*

Susan L. Miller, *Victims as Offenders: The Paradox of Women's Violence in Relationships*

Susan F. Sharp, *Hidden Victims: The Effects of the Death Penalty on Families of the Accused*

Robert H. Tillman and Michael L. Indergaard, *Pump and Dump: The Rancid Rules of the New Economy*

Mariana Valverde, *Law and Order: Images, Meanings, Myths*

Michael Welch, *Scapegoats of September 11th: Hate Crimes and State Crimes in the War on Terror*

Crime, Punishment, and Mental Illness

LAW AND THE BEHAVIORAL SCIENCES IN CONFLICT

PATRICIA E. ERICKSON
STEVEN K. ERICKSON

RUTGERS UNIVERSITY PRESS
New Brunswick, New Jersey, and London

Library of Congress Cataloging-in-Publication Data

Erickson, Patricia E., 1947–
    Crime, punishment, and mental illness : law and the behavioral
sciences in conflict / Patricia E. Erickson and Steven K. Erickson.
        p. ; cm.—(Critical issues in crime and society)
    Includes bibliographical references and index.
    ISBN 978-0-8135-4337-6 (hardcover : alk. paper)—
ISBN 978-0-8135-4338-3 (pbk. : alk. paper)
    1. Forensic psychiatry—United States.   2. Insanity (Law)—United
States.   3. Criminal responsibility—United States.   4. People with
mental disabilities and crime—United States.   I. Erickson, Steven K.,
1971–   II. Title.   III. Series.
    [DNLM: 1. Mental Disorders—psychology—United States.
2. Mentally Ill Persons—legislation & jurisprudence—United States.
3. Crime—psychology—United States.   4. Insanity Defense—United
States.   5. Mental Competency—United States.   6. Social Behavior—
United States. WM 33 AA1 E68 2008]
    RA1151.E72 2008
    614.'15—dc22
    2007044904

A British Cataloging-in-Publication record for this book is available
from the British Library.

Visit our Web site: http://rutgerspress.rutgers.edu

Manufactured in the United States of America

For Zachary Joseph Erickson

Contents

PREFACE

> You just loved crucifying me. You loved in-
> ducing cancer in my head, terrorizing my
> heart and ripping my soul all the time.
> —Virginia Tech killer Seung-Hui Cho *

As THIS BOOK was nearing completion, a twenty-three-year
old student at Virginia Polytechnic Institute, Seung-Hui Cho,
killed thirty-two people and wounded fifteen others before
committing suicide. The shootings took place on the Virginia
Tech campus on April 18, 2007, in two episodes. Cho first shot
two students in a dormitory; a few hours later he moved to a
classroom building where he killed five faculty members and
twenty-five more students before killing himself. In the ensuing
investigation, police found eight pages of notes in Cho's dorm
room that law enforcement characterized as a suicide note. The
note contained criticisms against people of privilege and Cho's
assertion that "you decided to spill my blood." On April 18, 2007,
NBC received a package from Cho time-stamped between the
first and second shootings. It contained, photos, writings, and
recorded videos in which Cho likened himself to Jesus Christ.

As the events unfolded at Virginia Tech, the shootings
received extensive media coverage. Media discourse routinely

---

*From the photographs, video, and writings that Seung-Hui Cho
mailed to NBC between the two attacks on the Virginia Tech campus
(http://www.msnbc.msn.com/id/18188852/).

emphasized information that indicated that Cho acted coolly and deliberately—the notes in his dorm, the package to NBC, the purchase of guns prior to the shootings, and witness accounts seemed to signify that Cho was a "cold-blooded killer." However, further investigation called into question Cho's mental state at the time of the shootings. Faculty and students interviewed after the shootings described Cho as a "loner," and some of Cho's professors reported being concerned about the content of his writings as well as his demeanor in classes. In fact, in 2005 two female students accused Cho of stalking and harassing them. The university investigated the matter and took Cho to a mental health facility for evaluation. The physician who examined Cho did not specify a diagnosis but indicated that Cho had a flat affect and depressed mood. He also noted that Cho denied suicidal thoughts and did not acknowledge symptoms of a thought disorder. Based on this mental health examination, the New River Community Services Board found him mentally ill and in need of hospitalization. Following Virginia state law, the board temporarily detained Cho at the mental health center pending a commitment hearing before the county district court. At the hearing, the judge certified in a court order that Cho presented an imminent danger to himself because of his mental illness, but recommended outpatient treatment for Cho rather than inpatient hospitalization. Cho never complied with the order for the mandated mental health treatments as an outpatient. No one monitored his compliance and no one ever summoned Cho to the court to ask why he failed to comply.

Cases like Cho's, in which a mentally ill individual commits acts of violence, form the central examples in this text as we examine the conflict between law and the behavioral sciences concerning treatment of the mentally ill in our society. These examples point to conflicts between law and the behavioral sciences for us to consider as we assess critically our public policy toward the mentally ill. However, the analysis of the text moves far beyond cases in which the mentally ill commit violent acts. For although events like the Virginia Tech shootings capture the media's attention and are tragic outcomes for victims and their families, acts of violence by the mentally ill are in actuality quite rare. However, they bring to the forefront questions about our society's response to the mentally ill. Questions we may ask include the following: Why did the judge permit Cho to remain among a student population after his psychiatric examination? Why was there no monitoring of Cho's compliance with the judge's order? Were the shootings the actions of a sane or insane person?

Answering these questions will require an understanding of how persons with mental illness have become primarily a criminal justice problem as reflected in laws and court decisions, as well as the movement to control the mentally ill through incarceration in prisons. The claim we will make throughout this text is that the social construction of mental illness as a criminal justice problem produces an incoherent public policy, one that is at odds with other moral and legal values of our society. Chapter 1 examines this issue by focusing on punishment, individual responsibility, and free will in terms of how these ideas relate to current policy and how they are at odds with empirical research offered by the behavioral sciences.

Chapter 2 examines and critically evaluates the transcarceration of the seriously mentally ill from asylums to prisons that resulted from deinstitutionalization. We will examine the consequences of deinstitutionalization and the strengths and weaknesses of recent laws designed to provide mechanisms to ensure that those persons remaining in the community are compliant with their medication and treatment programs.

Chapter 3 examines the different standards for competency that exist in criminal law versus the behavioral sciences, especially psychology, and the implications of these different standards for seriously mentally ill criminal defendants. The chapter also considers controversial issues regarding competency, including the use of forced medication to make a defendant competent to stand trial. Finally, the chapter takes a critical look at the issue of competency and the death penalty and asks why it should be unconstitutional to execute an incompetent prisoner.

In Chapter 4, we reflect on the problems created for seriously mentally ill defendants by the current legal conceptualization of the insanity defense. Our system of criminal law severely restricts the kinds and degrees of mental incapacity that qualify for this defense, and these limitations create specific problems for defendants. We present a critical discussion of the legal doctrine of insanity, focusing especially on the development of the defense in English common law. We also consider public misconceptions about the insanity defense and present insanity defense "reforms."

Chapter 5 considers what many scholars and legal practitioners consider a contradiction of our criminal system: our treatment of sex offenders who our legal system defines as "sexually violent predators." We prosecute and incarcerate these offenders even though our criminal justice system defines them as individuals who may suffer from a mental disease or mental abnormality. Current laws in most states also permit the involuntary civil commitment of these offenders following their incarceration. We review the debate concerning whether our current policy treats these sex offenders as both "bad" and "mad." In discussing this issue, we emphasize the special laws that exist concerning sex offenders, how these laws have changed over time, and whether these laws are consistent with the behavioral science research concerning the mental disorders of sex offenders.

Chapter 6 focuses on the criminalization of juvenile mentally ill offenders. We trace the evolution of the current juvenile justice system and critically evaluate recent changes in juvenile justice policy in which juvenile courts now process juvenile offenders in much the same way as adult criminal courts. Even absent mental illness, recent behavioral science research calls into question whether youths of varying ages have the same cognitive and emotional levels of development as adults. We explore the effects of this research in the context of mentally ill juveniles. As with mentally ill adults, we criminalize mentally ill juveniles, using juvenile detention facilities as the de facto asylums for youths with mental illness.

The final chapter reviews the themes raised in previous chapters to identify the dilemmas created by our current policies. We discuss guiding principles that we should use in formulating policy that are in harmony with larger societal values and how they might have made a difference to the cases described in the preceding chapters. One question recurs throughout the book: Does it matter that we criminalize mental illness, and if so, why?

ACKNOWLEDGMENTS

MANY PEOPLE CONTRIBUTED to the production of this book. In particular, we would like to thank Ray Michalowski and Adi Hovav at Rutgers University Press for their vision and encouragement. In addition, this book greatly benefited from the helpful insights and discussions over the years from Chuck Ewing, Michael Perlin, Bill Stuntz, Michelle Erickson, Rich Ciccone, and Steve Lamberti. We also thank Mike Khusid for his research assistance and Samantha Bell, Deborah Prohn, Ann Youmans, and Maureen Martens for their assistance in the preparation of the manuscript. Finally, Patricia Erickson thanks Canisius College for its support of the book through the Dean of Arts and Sciences Summer Grant Program.

Crime, Punishment,
and Mental Illness

CHAPTER 1

The Social Construction
of Mental Illness as a
Criminal Justice Problem

The courageous explanation is that the disease
affected his ability to tell right from wrong.
—Defense attorney William Difenderfer*

ON APRIL 28, 2000, Richard S. Baumham-
mer, a thirty-four-year-old immigration lawyer, got into his Jeep
with a .357 caliber handgun and a bag of shells. In seventy-
two minutes, five people were dead and one critically injured.
Baumhammer, who is white, shot his Jewish neighbor, two men
from India, and a black man as he drove his Jeep through sub-
urban Pittsburgh, Pennsylvania, stopping twice to vandalize
synagogues. After his arrest, the court determined that he was
mentally incompetent to stand trial and ordered him to May-
view State Hospital for treatment. Defense attorneys indicated
that once Baumhammer's mental health improved, they would
assert the insanity defense.

In the same year as the Baumhammer shootings, 2000, the
American Psychiatric Association published a new edition of

————

*Excerpt from the closing statement of defense counsel William Difend-
erfer to the jury on Wednesday, May 9, 2001 ("Man guilty" 2001).

I

the *Diagnostic and Statistical Manual of Mental Disorders* (*DSM*), the handbook used in diagnosing mental disorders. The disorders identified in the *DSM* do not identify a disorder called "insanity." Rather, insanity is a legal term with a definition that represents a moral conception of insanity and responsibility. In the Baumhammer shootings, the state of Pennsylvania defined insanity as a person acting under a "defect of reason" or "disease of the mind" and, consequently, unable to distinguish between right and wrong. With this definition, the emphasis is on the defendant's lack of understanding that the act is wrong. Mental health experts who testify at trial use relevant disorders listed in the *DSM* and the defendant's symptoms as evidence about the defendant's mental state. By matching the symptoms to the diagnostic descriptions within the *DSM,* mental health experts arrive at their diagnosis since there is no laboratory test that can test for the presence of the illness. In legal determinations of mental states, these experts analytically apply relevant diagnostic and clinical information to the specific legal issue. Usually the jury, but sometimes the trial judge, makes the determination as to whether the defendant is not guilty by reason of insanity.

At Baumhammer's trial, his attorneys admitted that he was the shooter but said that he was insane at the time of killings because of his delusional thinking. Psychiatrists for the defense testified that Baumhammer's beliefs tormented him and were the products of a mental illness. These beliefs included that the FBI and CIA were following him, that the family house cleaner was a spy, and that his skin was peeling off. In fact, Richard Baumhammer had a history of mental instability. For seven years, he received treatment from eight psychiatrists, and he once voluntarily committed himself to a psychiatric hospital for treatment. However, Baumhammer also, at times, neglected to take medication to control his delusions.

The prosecutor acknowledged that Baumhammer was mentally ill but said he was controlled, deliberate, calculating, and selective in picking out his victims while avoiding attention and successively eluding police. The psychiatrist who examined Baumhammer for the prosecution acknowledged that he suffered from several mental disorders, including antisocial personality disorder. He testified that Baumhammer showed no remorse or empathy for his victims and such symptoms are consistent with a diagnosis of antisocial personality disorder. He also diagnosed narcissism because Baumhammer, in the psychiatrist's opinion, was greatly concerned with his physical appearance and thought highly of himself.

The jury took just three hours to convict Baumhammer on five counts of first-degree murder, one count of attempted murder, and eight counts of ethnic intimidation. The jury also sentenced him to death although his lawyers are appealing his conviction ("Cold killer's 20-mile trail" 2000; "Man guilty" 2001).

CRIMINALIZING MENTAL ILLNESS

Why did the jury convict Baumhammer rather than finding him not guilty by reason of insanity? What is the role of mental health experts in criminal cases where the defendant is mentally ill? How does criminal law differ from behavioral science in terms of explanations for criminal behavior? Why do we incarcerate seriously mentally ill individuals who have committed crimes? We will examine these questions and others as we consider the contemporary response of American society to mentally ill persons who commit crimes. More specifically, we will examine our current policy of criminalizing mental illness, the reasons for the policy, and the problems our policy creates for the mentally ill and for our society.

The term "criminalization" refers to a process whereby agents of social control—legislators, police, district attorneys, and judges—impose a criminal rather than a psychiatric definition on an individual's behavior. It is a relabeling phenomenon in which the social control apparatus used to manage mental illness behavior becomes the criminal justice system rather than the mental health system (Fisher, Silver, and Wolff 2006, 545). In the *Baumhammer* case, we can identify at least two points that indicate reliance on the criminal justice system rather than the mental health system. First, there was the lack of continuing and perhaps involuntary psychiatric care for Richard Baumhammer that may have prevented the shootings, and second, there was the state's restrictive definition for insanity that resulted in incarceration rather than treatment and confinement in a mental hospital.

In the United States, research derived from a variety of sources points to the criminalization of mental illness by demonstrating an increasingly disproportionate presence of individuals with mental disorders, especially serious mental disorders, in various sectors of the criminal justice system. In 1992, the National Alliance for the Mentally Ill (NAMI) and the Public Citizen's Health Research Group released a report that described alarmingly high numbers of people with schizophrenia, bipolar disorder, and other severe mental illnesses incarcerated in jails across the country. The report documented that most of the mentally ill arrested had not committed major crimes but rather misdemeanors or minor felonies directly related to the symptoms of their untreated illnesses. A report by the U.S. Department of Justice in 1999, based on a survey of inmates, indicated that 16 percent of all inmates in state and federal jails and prisons had schizophrenia, bipolar illness, major depression, or another severe illness (Ditton 1999). This meant that on any given day there were approximately 283,000 persons with severe mental illnesses incarcerated in federal and state prisons. In contrast, there were approximately 70,000 persons with severe mental illnesses in public psychiatric hospitals (National Alliance for the Mentally Ill 2003, 2).

The policy of criminalization of the mentally ill continues into the twenty-first century. A 2006 report by the U.S. Department of Justice indicates that by midyear 2005 more than half of all prison and jail inmates reported symptoms that indicated that they had a mental health problem (56 percent of state prisoners, 45 percent of federal prisoners, and 64 percent of jail inmates). The study measured the presence of mental health problems by asking inmates about a recent history of mental health problems or symptoms of mental disorders that occurred in the last year. Based on this measure, the study concluded that the mental health problems reported were serious in nature. More than two-fifths of state prisoners and more than half of jail inmates reported symptoms that met the criteria for mania. About 23 percent of state prisoners and 30 percent of jail inmates reported symptoms of major depression. An estimated 15 percent of state prisoners and 24 percent of jail inmates reported symptoms that met the criteria for a psychotic disorder (James and Glaze 2006).

Moreover, mental health problems are more likely among certain categories of individuals in the criminal justice system. Both the 1999 and 2006 report by the U.S. Department of Justice found that female inmates had higher rates of mental health problems than males. The researchers also found that prevalence of mental health problems also varied by racial or ethnic group. White inmates had higher rates of reported mental health problems than African Americans or Hispanics In addition, both the 1999 and 2006 study by the U.S. Department of Justice point to some important background characteristics of mentally ill inmates. They found that homelessness in the year before incarceration was more common among inmates who had mental health problems, as was living in a foster home while growing up and experiencing sexual and physical abuse as a child (Ditton 1999, 3–4; James and Glaze 2006, 4–5). In order to understand the prevalence of mental illness in jails and prisons and among certain categories of inmates, we must examine how mental illness behavior became a social problem for the criminal justice system to manage and control.

CRIMINALIZING MENTAL ILLNESS
AS A SOCIAL CONSTRUCTION

The criminalization of mental illness reflects a social construction about the meaning of mental illness that is substantially different from how we interpreted mental illness in an earlier period in American society when we considered mental illness as primarily a medical problem often requiring prolonged hospitalization in state-run mental institutions. Identifying mental illness as socially constructed means that we examine how social forces shape our understanding of and actions toward mental illness and the mentally ill. Social constructionists recognize the effects of such social forces as language, culture, politics, professional structures, and norms in shaping the knowledge base that produces our interpretations of phenomena (Maines 2000; Hacking 1999; Perinbanayagam 1986; Berger and Luckman 1966). This book examines how social forces shape our response toward the mentally ill who commit crimes.

Identifying the criminalization of mental illness as a social construction also means that purposive action by individuals and groups create the social response toward the mentally ill. Consequently, at various times, the social construction of mental illness and the mentally ill changes because of the interpretation given to it by influential labelers—individuals and groups who criticize the current interpretation and offer a convincing rationale for its change (Goode 1994; Spector and Kitsuse 1977; Becker 1963). Indeed, social constructionists would point to the complex but essentially reciprocal relationship between the criminal justice and mental health systems over time (Thompson 2005, 1). As we will discuss more fully in the following chapters, increased hospital admissions occur in eras of fewer jail and prison admissions, and decreased hospital admissions occur when jail and prison populations increase (Harcourt 2006; Liska et al. 1999; Torrey et al. 1992; Teplin 1984; Steadman, Monahan et al.1984; Grabosky

1980; Rothman 1971). This means that generally, if prison populations are large, the mental hospital population is relatively small; the reverse also tends to be true.

Finally, social constructionists emphasize the importance of "unmasking" our taken-for-granted reality to see its consequences, both intended and unintended. For example, in both social constructions—prisons and mental hospitals—we use coercive control over the mentally ill in an effort to modify their behavior. In seeing the similarity between the two kinds of institutions, sociologist Erving Goffman (1961/1990) described how both the prison and mental hospital qualified as examples of "total institutions." He explained that in total institutions there is a split between a group of inmates or patients removed from the outside world and a staff integrated with the outside world. Goffman maintained that we achieve control in both the prison and mental hospital through confinement and exclusion. However, while Goffman described important points of similarity between the prison and mental hospital, it is important to understand that the socially constructed meaning of mental illness is very different in these two institutions. When we interpret mental illness as a medical problem, confinement to a mental hospital serves the goal of treatment because of an underlying societal value of compassion for a person who has an illness. Alternatively, when we interpret mental illness as a criminal justice problem, confinement serves the goals of incapacitation because of the underlying value of keeping the community safe from someone who has committed a crime.

In sum, how we "frame" our response to the mentally ill is dependent upon which values and consequent goals take priority in shaping our public policy. In both the prison and hospital response, we define mental illness as a social problem; however, the value of incapacitation and the goal of community safety frame the issue very differently than the value of compassion and goal of treatment. Once constructed, we tend to "freeze" our interpretations of mental illness and the mentally ill within the socially constructed framework. For example, under the current criminalization-of-mental-illness construction, we react to a claim of mental illness by a person who has committed a crime with suspicion. A common reaction is that the person is malingering and even able to fool psychiatrists and psychologists.

This book examines the debate over which systems should primarily control our response to the mentally ill when we have concerns about the criminal behavior of the mentally ill. It considers how social constructions shape this debate and the role of the debate in formulating and implementing our policies toward the mentally ill. In the forthcoming chapters, we argue that two social constructions account for our current public policy that gives the criminal justice system primary control over the mentally ill. One social construction about mental illness that forms a major theme of his book concerns a long-standing debate and disagreement between criminal law and behavioral science concerning the appropriate model that American society should use when considering how to respond to mentally ill individuals who commit crimes (Green 1995). Another way to state this issue is that criminal law is ambivalent about the role of behavioral science in the criminal justice system. This ambivalence arises because the systems of criminal law and behavioral science have fundamental differences concerning their assumptions about behavior and, in the case of mental illness, how law should respond in situations when the mental state of a person is at issue in deciding the person's responsibility for a criminal act.

A second social construction that is a major theme of the book concerns the negative public sentiment and punitive policy toward the mentally ill that began to take shape in the late 1970s and flourishes today. This second construction developed from reframing mental illness as a failure of individual responsibility rather than an illness requiring a humane orientation and medical intervention (Pustilnik 2005). Reframing mental illness as a failure of individual responsibility, along with a continuation of the traditional criminal law model, created a shift to a punitive stance toward the mentally ill—hence, the criminalization of mental illness.

In the following chapters, we will examine in more detail the reframing of mental illness as a criminal justice problem by considering legal issues, behavioral science research, and proposals for reform of the criminalization approach. However, before we turn our attention to these issues, we will examine in more detail the two social constructions, just described, that gave rise to the criminalization of mental illness: (1) the law's ambivalence about the role of the behavioral sciences in the criminal process and (2) the conception of mental illness as moral failure requiring punishment.

The Law's Ambivalence about Behavioral Science

The *Baumhammer* case illustrates how criminal law and the behavioral sciences interact when the mental state of a defendant is an issue. In trials where the issue is the insanity of the defendant at the time of the crime, our adversary system permits experts to testify for both the prosecution and defense concerning the defendant's mental state. However, more noteworthy in characterizing the interaction between law and behavioral science is the ambivalence in legal scholarship and in criminal proceedings about the role, or more accurately the power, that the behavioral sciences exert in criminal proceedings. Perlin (1994), a legal scholar and an outspoken critic of the policy of criminalization of mental illness, argues that we are apprehensive about the consequences that would result from an increased role for the behavioral sciences. This apprehension about possible consequences arises from the fact that criminal law and the behavioral sciences operate in two very different socially constructed worlds. These differing social constructions have different assumptions and approaches for explaining criminal behavior and different agendas regarding policy toward mentally ill offenders. Giving the behavioral sciences an increased role would by necessity change the social construction of our system of criminal law by allowing behavioral science a greater influence within the legal system.

One way to think about the socially constructed reality of criminal law is to consider the social meaning that we attach to it as it currently exists in American society. As illustrated in *Baumhammer*, and in other examples that we will describe in forthcoming chapters, criminal law and law generally place great emphasis on the philosophical tradition of moral reasoning as well as on religious ideas concerning good and evil. From these traditions arose the assumption that all people possess free will and that we could and should understand behavior as an outcome of choices persons make as free agents (Green 1995; Bazelon 1983). In contrast, the behavioral sciences that include psychiatry and psychology are grounded in a deterministic and empirical tradition and, therefore, examine the causes or reasons for behavior in terms of a person's social, psychological, and biological history and, in addition, in terms of the influence of social structure (D'Angelo 1968; Furlong 1981). Behavioral scientists do not identify free will as a construct that they can measure within the personality of an individual, and consequently the behavioral sciences do not consider it as an explanatory factor of human behavior. The behavioral sciences may examine what factors in the person's background explain their actions or conduct in a given situation, but this is a very different idea than "free will." Responses to the factors in a person's background suggest a great deal of variability among people in terms of explaining their actions or conduct in a given situation.

Our criminal law tradition recognizes that social, psychological, and biological forces over which an individual may have little or no control may influence the person's behavior.

However, the tradition still maintains that persons retain sufficient intentionality or rationality over their behavior—except in extreme situations such as the defense of insanity or in crimes committed by children—to act "freely." The law's emphasis on free will derives from its historical moral framework regarding how to evaluate whether a person is blameworthy for a criminal act. Generally, the law defines a person as blameworthy through the constructs of *mens rea* ("guilty mind") and *actus reus* ("wrongful act"). As with the idea of free will, these constructs developed under English common law through the influence of religious thinking about evil and sin. Today our system of criminal law retains the concepts of *mens rea* and *actus reus* as essential elements of most crimes. Blameworthiness, from a legal point of view, is the concurrence of *mens rea* and *actus reus*. More commonly, we say, for example, that a person is guilty of murder if the person killed an individual (*actus reus*) with malice aforethought (*mens rea*). This brings the idea of free will to the forefront because malice indicates intentionality and evilness. The assumption of free will, coupled with the moral framework embodied in the constructs of *mens rea* and *actus reus,* permits us to affix blame in terms of punishment for the crime committed. Legal definitions of insanity such as that applied in the Baumhammer trial specify what would constitute an absence of free will. In *Baumhammer,* the definition of insanity concerned the inability to discern right from wrong because of mental disease or defect.

From a behavioral science point of view, the preceding "free will" analysis is an artificial and outdated one, viewed through a distorted lens, because *mens rea* and *actus reus* are not factors that are thought to explain behavior: they are religious/moral conceptions concerning the nature of good and evil. Behavioral science examines the world of empirically observable constructs, known as "variables." The purpose of empirical observation in the behavioral sciences is to understand and predict behavior.

The variables examined by behavioral science present a complex view of human behavior, expressed as theories. Systematic empirical investigation is necessary to decide whether theoretical ideas are valid. Moreover, the behavioral sciences view mental illnesses as diseases that have biological and psychological causes. In some types of mental disorders, a person's mental state will deteriorate as the disease progresses. The symptoms displayed by a person with mental illness are outward manifestations of a specific illness located within the brain.

In situations in which a person with a mental disorder commits a criminal act, one role of the psychiatrist and psychologist is to assess, to the extent possible, the role of the mental illness in producing the criminal act. Consequently, the behavioral science paradigm does not consider the issue of blameworthiness as a goal of scientific inquiry. Rather, the behavioral science paradigm would see prevention of criminal behaviors through treatment of mental illness as the focus. Since the reason for criminal behavior is difficult to ascertain, retribution is often considered an illegitimate purpose of punishment from a behavioral science point of view. Rehabilitation and perhaps even deterrence are more appropriate purposes of punishment because the behavioral science view suggests that we may be able to change a person's behavior if we change the person's environment or, in the case of a mentally ill individual, provide appropriate medication and psychotherapy. Essential to this theory is the belief that behavior can be changed through mental health interventions and such treatments are preferable over policies favoring only incapacitation or retribution. Therefore, the principles of behavioral science appear to cut across the powerful forces of punishment in the criminal justice process. Punishment serves to express profound feelings of social disapproval and condemnation. In contrast, psychological principles reflect a utilitarian attitude toward criminal behavior committed by the mentally ill.

FOCUS 1.1. TYPES OF MENTALLY ILL OFFENDERS

Throughout the following chapters, we will focus on the issue of criminalizing mental illness, although we recognize that mental illness is not the causal reason that explains all criminal behavior committed by mentally ill offenders. Hiday (1999) classifies three categories of mentally ill offenders. One category includes those persons who are homeless and have co-occurring mental illness and substance abuse. These individuals may shoplift or commit other minor crimes in order to survive. Torrey's (1997) discussion of the consequences of deinstitutionalization, discussed in this chapter, largely describes these mentally ill individuals. A second category includes persons who have serious mental illness but who offend because of their antisocial personalities that are independent of their serious mental illness. These individuals may show little remorse when they commit crimes (antisocial personality), but the criminal act has little to do with, for example, their depression. A third category includes individuals who commit violent crimes as a direct result of their mental illness. Notice in the *Baumhammer* case, discussed at the beginning of this chapter, there is a difference of opinion among the expert witnesses concerning whether the killings were a direct result of Baumhammer's mental illness or, alternatively, whether Baumhammer's antisocial personality was the explanatory factor. The issue becomes more complex because the DSM lists antisocial personality as a disorder; however, most behavioral scientists do not include it within their understanding of mental illness.

In sum, the socially constructed world of the behavioral sciences relies upon the scientific method in addressing criminal behaviors. This method relies on empirical measurement and emphasizes the mutable propensity of behavior for its interpretations about criminal behavior. It is also assumes a causal model of human behavior. Key to this model is the idea that complex behaviors can be reduced to measurable constructs which can be assessed with empirical methods. When considering mental illness and criminal behavior, the behavioral scientist will investigate the role of mental illness in producing the criminal behavior in question and provide a causal explanation for such behavior that appropriate mental health interventions may prevent in the future. In contrast, criminal law traces its social origin to the assumptions and religious values embodied in English common law that depend on a view of the person as a responsible agent who exercises free will when committing acts of wrongdoing. This model of criminal law is comfortable with punishing the mentally ill because it presumes that people are able to behave according to the legally ascribed codes of conduct. Accordingly, it belongs to the tradition that values retribution. Therefore, we can say that criminal law and the behavioral sciences wear two different social masks that represent their socially constructed worlds. When both masks interact in situations where mental illness and criminal behavior are present, each may want their socially constructed world to prevail.

The Conception of Mental Illness as
Moral Failure Requiring Punishment

A second social construction about the criminalization of the mentally ill concerns the emphasis on the punitive approach as our society's response to the mentally ill. Pustilnik (2005) argues that in order to understand this emphasis, we must understand that the prevailing social meaning of mental illness is one of moral failure, not a set of medical conditions that require medical treatment. The public perceives people with mental ill-nesses, not uniformly but predominantly, as culpably failing to conform to a core social norm: personal responsibility. This asso-ciation of mental illness with failure of personal responsibility makes it appear rational to punish the mentally ill. Consequently, the moral/punitive model now is our dominant response to mental illness and the medical/therapeutic model is a second-ary response. The role of the criminal justice system is to punish culpable failures of responsibility. Prison is the place for people who violate the core social norm of personal responsibility. The mentally ill are now included as violators of core social norms.

How did such a social construction develop? In part, it occurred because of deinstitutionalization, the process of mov-ing severely mentally ill people out of large state mental hospi-tals into communities for treatment that began in the 1950s and 1960s but took firm hold in the 1970s. Deinstitutionalization occurred for several reasons that we will discuss more fully in chapter 2. However, to understand the shift to interpreting men-tal illness as a failure of personal responsibility, it is important to understand that during the 1960s and 1970s, the hospital-ized mentally ill and their advocates sought legal rights based on autonomy and a libertarian ideal of governmental regulation of behavior. Both in the courts and through legislation, the focus was on limiting the criteria for involuntary civil commitment into mental hospitals and, instead, to provide access to treatment within communities. Advocates for the rights of the mentally ill claimed that communities could provide the care that the mentally ill needed instead of relying on centralized institutions, which often provided custody but little compassionate care. This emphasis on the rights of the mentally ill occurred in a political climate that emphasized the primacy of individual rights and personal autonomy, not only for mentally ill persons but for all citizens. In the 1960s and 1970s, social movements such as the civil rights movement and the women's movement emphasized the need for equal rights and the need for government to intervene to provide those rights. For the mentally ill, involuntary civil commitment laws and court decisions from the 1960s to the late 1970s changed dramatically in favor of the rights of the mentally ill (Perlin 2000; Torrey 1997).

One consequence of the assertion for rights and freedom from involuntary civil confinement was the corollary expectation that the mentally ill would seek mental health treatment in their community and that such treatment would be readily available. Such beliefs built upon the ideas that mental illnesses were treatable and that mental health approaches to these behaviors were effective in controlling socially undesirable behaviors. Treatment would result in the mentally ill conforming to societal norms because it was firmly presumed that illegal behaviors were mainly the products of their mental illness. To a significant extent, that expectation did not occur. Psychiatrist E. Fuller Torrey (1997), an outspoken critic of deinstitutionalization and an advocate for the mentally ill, describes deinstitutionalization as a psychiatric *Titanic,* the major contributing factor to the criminalization of mental illness. Torrey describes several factors that created the criminalization crisis. First, most of those moved from the nation's public psychiatric hospitals were severely mentally ill, requiring medication and rehabilitation services. Second, hospitals discharged patients without ensuring that they received the medication and rehabilitation services necessary for them to live successfully in the community. Third, once the public hospitals closed, there were no services available for people who later became seriously mentally ill and who would benefit from long-term hospitalization. Fourth, it was presumed that the mentally ill would seek community treatment despite established clinical knowledge that many severely mentally ill people fail to discern their own behaviors as affected by mental illness. Consequently, in the late 1970s and the 1980s, the mentally ill became a significant part of the homeless population. Substance abuse, failure to take psychotropic medications, and criminal acts, usually minor, frequently accompanied homelessness and gained public attention. Media accounts drew attention to the homeless mentally ill and emphasized accounts of violence by mentally ill persons released into the community. The "visibility" of the mentally ill created an image before the public and to agents of social control as persons failing to control themselves. This view united with the important societal norm of individual responsibility presented a rationale for a criminal justice response in lieu of the response of the mental health system.

Often at the heart of arguments about the mentally ill in this new social construction is the notion that many mental illnesses are not real phenomena. From this viewpoint, "illness" is merely a label applied to people who commit blameworthy acts rather than a set of real and treatable medical conditions distinct from simple bad behavior. A variation of this claim is that it is easy to fake mental illness, and people often do so in order to escape the criminal justice process. Such beliefs are understandable given the increased acceptance within the criminal justice system that illegal behaviors often result from mental illnesses such as alcohol and drug abuse, which are presumed volitional by most people and our legal traditions. Granting parole for inmates who undertake drug counseling and mandating such counseling for probationers gave the appearance that criminal behaviors conducted under the influence of alcohol or drugs was a product of mental illness and not a wrongful choice by the actor. A third underlying argument is that once we make exceptions for the mentally ill, we create a slippery slope that will enable other types of offenders to offer "excuses" for behavior to escape the criminal justice process. The numerous novel insanity and diminished-capacity defenses such as battered women's syndrome gave credence to the fear that the behavioral sciences were excusing behaviors never before conceived as products of a mentally ill mind.

FOCUS 1.2. THE CONTINUING DEBATE
CONCERNING FREE WILL VERSUS DETERMINISM

The debate about free will and determinism in criminal law continues to generate controversy among scholars. Most recently, the highly regarded journal *Behavioral Sciences and the Law* devoted an entire issue to the subject. Noted legal scholars, psychologists, and neuroscientists presented their views on the subject. At one extreme is the claim of psychologist and legal scholar Stephen Morse who argues, "Free will plays no role in the positive criteria for criminal responsibility" (2007, 211). At the other extreme lies the claim of neuroscientists Burns and Bechara who state, "Much of what we know already about these brain mechanisms indicates that decision-making is greatly influenced by implicit processes that do not necessarily reach consciousness" (2007, 263–64). For a further discussion of this issue, see *Behavioral Sciences and the Law,* vol. 25.

In sum, beginning in the 1970s, the social construction of mental illness began to change in the direction of indicating a defect of morality or will, a culpable failure to conform one's behavior to the social norm of personal responsibility. This social construction made it appear rational to reinforce the responsibility norm by punishing the mentally ill. Recently, criminologists have pointed to the fact that retribution (in contrast to deterrence and rehabilitation) has gained prominence as the most important justification for punishment, for all criminals not only the incarcerated mentally ill. Again, the emphasis placed on individual responsibility explains the prominence of retribution. If the criminal act reflects the free will of the person and the person's evil or sinful character, then retribution is the response that demonstrates society's power over the individual, and it is the penalty called for to pay for the evil act. Given the dramatic rise of violent crime during the 1960s and 1980s, the resurgence of retribution seems comprehensible. The emphasis on retribution stands in contrast to the reliance on rehabilitation and deterrence of earlier eras.

Incarceration of the mentally ill has created several dilemmas for correctional facilities. First, as we will discuss in later chapters, prisons have become the de facto asylums for the mentally ill. However, research also indicates that prisons are not equipped to deal with this population. Appropriate medication and psychotherapy is often not available and is not viewed as appropriate for criminals (Beck and Maruschak 2001). Correctional officers may not receive proper training on how to handle seriously mentally ill prisoners. Several reported cases of the use of improper restraints resulting in the death of mentally ill prisoners have created concern about the incarceration of these prisoners. Mentally ill prisoners placed in solitary confinement because of psychotic behavior frequently commit suicide, a phenomenon discussed more fully in chapter 2.

Incarceration of the mentally ill has shifted our focus as a society from the offender's mental illness to the problems involved in the management and containment of them. It serves to express community condemnation of wrongdoers, especially the mentally ill wrongdoers whom we may fear the most, and in this sense the punishment focus may serve an important social purpose by providing for a sort of collective catharsis. When we hear accounts of violent behavior by mentally ill inmates, our desire for safety takes precedence over notions about any unmet psychiatric needs of that inmate. The criminalization of the mentally ill removes the issue from the outside world and places it behind locked doors. However, while such a socially constructed reality might provide us with some degree of safety, it also gives us a conflicted and confused social order because our

FOCUS 1.3. THE CHALLENGE TO NOTIONS OF
FREE WILL AND DETERMINISM

A team of scientists reported that a gene may help explain
why some children exposed to violence, neglect, and abuse
become violent adults while others growing up in the same
type of environment do not become violent adults. The
claim of the scientists is that the findings provide new evidence for what will prove to be incredibly controversial: the
genetics of personality, behavior, and social interactions.

The twenty-six-year study involved 442 male New
Zealanders who researchers followed from birth. The gene
discovered makes an enzyme called monoamine oxidase
A that cleans up excess neurotransmitters, chemical mes-
sengers that allow brain cells to communicate. Researchers
found that children who grow up in homes that are psychologically, physically, or sexually abusive have a ninefold
increased risk of becoming antisocial adults if they had a
low-performing version of the MAOA gene rather than a
normal version. Those individuals not exposed to maltreat-
ment who had the low-performing gene were not at higher
risk. The researchers also found that the gene has a protective effect because boys who grow up in troubled homes
but have normal or above normal copies of the MAOA
gene generally do not become criminals (Caspi et al. 2002).

treatment of the mentally ill is inconsistent with other important societal values.

THE CONFLICTED AND CONFUSED SOCIAL ORDER

The major theme of this book is to examine critically the
confusion that we have created by criminalizing mental illness

and to explore the reasons why it is important to change current policy. As we will describe more fully in the next chapters, the confused and conflicted social order negatively affects not only the mentally ill but also the criminal justice system, the mental health system, and society. While the negative impact on the mentally ill and the criminal justice and mental health systems may be more readily apparent, criminalization affects society in several ways. First, victims and their families who experience criminal acts by the mentally ill might have experienced a different outcome had our public policy been different. Incidents such as the Virginia Tech and the Baumhammer shootings are largely preventable. Second, the mentally ill, as members of our society, deserve effective and compassionate treatment, and such treatment is especially important for those whose illnesses will worsen without treatment. Third, those who work in our jails and prisons often confront seriously mentally ill individuals but are not equipped or trained to deal with their behavior. Changing policy in favor of a strong mental health policy makes it less likely that mentally ill individuals will wind up in the criminal justice system.

In the forthcoming chapters, we identify how the medical/ therapeutic model of the mentally ill creates strain when placed against the current moral/punitive model. Perlin (1994), a legal scholar and critic of our current policy, conceptualizes this strain as a division within our minds. He maintains that we have competing urges to explain causally (the model of the behavioral sciences) and to attach blame (the model of criminal law) to the mentally ill. These powerful urges mean that we tend to have cyclical and sector-based policies: humane treatment of the mentally ill reflects the dominance of the medical/therapeutic model, while criminalization of the mentally ill reflects the dominance of the moral/punitive model. This mental division is possible because our legal consciousness—our ideas about the nature, function, and operation of law—is not only determined by law. It is one of the many competing forces that shape our consciousness about assumptions and categories that we use to make sense of our social life and its corresponding social order. In addition to law, our legal consciousness contains our social norms and values, including social norms and values that offer competing claims of social life and social order (Engel 1998). The norms and values of science and the treatment and rehabilitation model are among these competing claims.

Recent developments in the behavioral sciences concerning the biological basis for many mental disorders make it highly likely that the confusion and conflicts that we have about mental illness and criminal law will escalate and become more intense. An additional goal of this book is to offer a perspective that can reconnect criminal law with the behavioral sciences in ways that make sense given both our moral values and developments in the behavioral sciences. We want research to inform criminal law but not take its place. We want research to provoke us all to rethink our policy of criminalization of mentally ill in favor of a policy that emphasizes coherence, crime prevention, and treatment of the mentally ill.

CHAPTER 2

Systems of Social Control

FROM ASYLUMS TO PRISONS

I felt a sensation, like something was enter-
ing me. . . . I got the urge to push, shove or
sidekick. As the train was coming, the feeling
disappeared and came back. . . . I pushed the
woman who had blond hair.

—Andrew Goldstein*

ON JANUARY 3, 1999, during the evening rush
hour, Andrew Goldstein, a man with a long history of schizophrenia, waited anxiously for the next subway to arrive at the
Twenty-third Street station in Manhattan. Also waiting was a
young receptionist, Kendra Webdale, a recent transplant from her
hometown of Buffalo, New York. Suddenly, as the subway rushed
into the station, Goldstein shoved Webdale onto the tracks, where
she was killed instantly. Goldstein quietly waited for the police
arrive and was booked that night for the murder.

As the days and months went by, many questioned how
such an event could happen. A *New York Times* article on May
23, 1999, reported that hundreds of psychiatrists, therapists, and
social workers had treated Andrew Goldstein, and these mental
health professionals knew he was dangerous. More specifically, in

---

*Excerpts from Andrew Goldstein's confession (Michael Winerip,
"Bedlam in the Streets," *New York Times,* May 23, 1999).

the two years before Goldstein killed Webdale, he had attacked at least thirteen other people and had been repeatedly hospitalized for his chronic schizophrenia. However, hospital staff members kept treating and discharging him even though they knew that he repeatedly attacked strangers in public places. They also knew Goldstein was dangerous because he had attacked them—two psychiatrists, a nurse, a social worker, and a therapy aide in two years' time. However, for each hospitalization—there were thirteen in 1997 and 1998 alone—physicians prescribed Goldstein medication and then discharged him, often after just a few days, to live on his own in a basement apartment. Particularly chilling was Goldstein's hospitalization six months before Webdale's death, after striking another woman he did not know on a New York subway.

The *New York Times* article also reported that sometimes well-meaning police officers delivered Andrew Goldstein to the hospital. More often, however, he walked into the psychiatric emergency room on his own, seeking help. Six weeks before he killed Webdale, Goldstein arrived at Jamaica Hospital in Queens, again seeking hospitalization. He walked into the emergency room complaining of hearing voices, sure that people were following him, and with the belief that people were living in him. Goldstein's last hospitalization before attacking Webdale was from November 24 to December 15. Two weeks into his hospitalization, on December 9, Goldstein's psychiatrist was still describing him as disorganized, thought disordered, and very delusional. However, the discharge team had already set his release for the next week. On December 15, the hospital discharged him with a week's supply of medicine and a form advising him to report to a counseling center.

Goldstein's principal defense at his trial was insanity. His first trial ended in a hung jury. At his second trial, a jury convicted him of second-degree murder, rejecting his insanity claim. On appeal, New York State's highest court, the Court of Appeals, reversed his conviction and ordered a new trial because of hearsay evidence used by the prosecution's expert psychiatrist in testifying at trial (*People v. Goldstein,* 873 N.E. 2d 727 [N.Y. 2005]). Rather than face a new trial, Goldstein pled guilty to manslaughter, receiving a sentence of twenty-three years in prison with five years of postrelease supervision, including mandatory psychiatric treatment upon release. A *New York Times* article on October 11, 2006, reported that at his court appearance for the plea, he submitted a *written* statement to the judge stating, "I looked to see if the train was coming down the tracks. I saw that the subway train was coming into the station. When the train was almost in front of us, I placed my hands on the back of her shoulders and pushed her. My actions caused her to fall onto the tracks."

Deinstitutionalization as a Social Experiment

Understanding the *Goldstein* case begins with asking why hospitals kept discharging him even though he was seriously mentally ill and violent. The answer to this question lies with current mental health policy, more specifically the deinstitutionalization of America's psychiatric hospitals and the replacement of those hospitals with community mental health centers. Deinstitutionalization began in the 1950s and took firm hold in the 1960s and 1970s, dramatically changing the shape of mental health care for the seriously mentally ill. Rather than a seriously mentally ill patient staying indefinitely in state hospitals, public policy required either treatment in the community or release into the community after brief periods of hospitalization. As Goldstein's treatment illustrates, the proponents of deinstitutionalization assumed that mentally ill individuals would take prescribed medications and seek out patient counseling. Unfortunately, such assumptions sometimes lead to tragic outcomes such as the killing of Kendra Webdale. More typically, deinstitutionalization created a climate that was less tolerant of the

FOCUS 2.1. DEINSTITUTIONALIZATION INTO
COUNTY JAILS: THE CASE OF MICHAEL T. BENNETT

Hundreds of newspaper articles have reported on the transcarceration of the mentally ill into America's jails. The *Buffalo News* reported on July 22, 2002, that the Erie County Holding Center had become one of the biggest mental institutions in the region, setting aside one hundred beds for mentally ill inmates. The one hundred beds represented roughly one-sixth of the jail's capacity. The county reported spending close to $200,000 a year to medicate the inmates and thousands more for psychiatric counseling. In documenting the problems produced by transcarceration, the article described the case of Michael T. Bennett, a diagnosed paranoid schizophrenic, who police found walking naked down a lower west side street. Bennett fought with officers when they tried to take him into custody. On his third day in jail, Bennett died after repeatedly jumping off his bed headfirst into the bars of his cell.

mentally ill and more willing to use prisons and jails as their place of confinement.

The Magnitude of Deinstitutionalization and Its Stated Rationale

Deinstitutionalization is a formal policy of the federal government. President John F. Kennedy first articulated deinstitutionalization as a direction for public policy in 1960 and 1961 and then proclaimed it a political goal in 1963. In 1961, the Joint Commission on Mental Illness and Health's Action for Mental Health claimed that long-term stays in hospitals produced institutionalized behavior and a tendency toward chronic illness.

Moreover, hospitals were extremely costly and were little more than large-scale custodial warehouses. The commission recommended preventing hospitalization, curtailing its length when it was unavoidable, and returning patients to community life, where ideally they would receive treatment through community-based services. President Jimmy Carter's Commission on Mental Health further elaborated that deinstitutionalization had "the objective of maintaining the greatest degree of freedom, self-determination, autonomy, dignity, and integrity of body, mind, and spirit for the individual while he or she participates in treatment or receives services" (Torrey 1997, 10–11). This principle, treating the seriously mentally ill in the least restrictive setting, found support in federal and state legislation as well as in the courts (Rose 1979, 430–31). It also found support in judicial rulings at the state and federal levels starting in the early 1960s.

Psychiatrist E. Fuller Torrey describes the magnitude of deinstitutionalization, claiming that it qualifies as one of the largest social experiments in American history. He notes that in 1955, there were 558,239 severely mentally ill patients in the nation's public psychiatric hospitals. In 1994, this number had been reduced to 71,619. Keep in mind that the count of 558,239 patients in public psychiatric hospitals in 1955 was in relationship to the nation's total population at the time, which was 164 million. By 1994, the nation's population had increased to 260 million. If there had been the same proportion of patients in the population in mental hospitals in 1994 as there had been in 1955, the number of patients would have totaled 885,010. Therefore, the true magnitude of deinstitutionalization is the difference between 885,010 and 71,619. Approximately 92 percent of the people who would have been living in public psychiatric hospitals in 1955 were not living in them in 1994 (Torrey 1997, 8–9).

Torrey also points out that deinstitutionalization resulted in the discharge of the most seriously mentally ill from the nation's public psychiatric hospitals. Schizophrenia was the diagnosis for between 50 and 60 percent of patients. Manic-depressive illness and severe depression was the diagnosis for 10 to 15 percent and organic brain diseases—epilepsy, strokes, Alzheimer's disease, and brain damage secondary to trauma were the diagnoses for an additional 10 to 15 percent. The remaining individuals residing in public psychiatric hospitals had conditions such as mental retardation with psychosis, autism, and other psychiatric disorders of childhood, and alcoholism and drug addiction with concurrent brain damage (Torrey 1997, 10–11).

This decline in the state hospital population represented a reversal of a long-standing trend, a radical transformation in the treatment of the seriously mentally ill. Since the turn of the twentieth century, state hospital populations had grown steadily, increasing fourfold from 1903 to 1955 (Gronfein 1985; Kramer 1977). The growth of state mental hospitals followed the emerging public hygiene movement, which saw health as a public enterprise and, therefore, a function of the government. Prior to this movement, psychiatric patients were often on their own, with only the wealthy able to afford private psychiatric treatment at exclusive hospitals such as the world-renowned McLean hospital outside of Boston. In addition, the numbers of mentally ill in asylums dramatically increased due to the migration of millions of Americans from rural farmlands to the burgeoning cities. Urban life called to attention deviant behaviors previously tolerated in rural communities. Migration to urban life also intensified poverty and the accompanying social problems, including mental illness. States designed mental hospitals first as a place of safety for the mentally ill and second as a place for treatment (Goldman 1983).

Constructing the Critique of the Asylum

Although asylums had a therapeutic function, these publicly supported state mental hospitals also had a clear containment function that at times dominated the therapeutic objective. Sociologist William Gronfein (1985) describes asylums as depositories as well as hospitals, receptacles into which the community could place those individuals whose presence in civil society had become intolerable. The legal procedure of involuntary civil commitment, which was by far the most common admissions procedure until the 1960s, guaranteed that the community could maintain civil order by using permissive legal procedures to compel patients to accept treatment, whatever wishes the patients themselves may have. Gronfein also characterizes how involuntary commitment placed the state hospitals under compulsion as well as the patient because hospitals were constrained to accept all those persons who had been committed for treatment. Hospital administrators also had to be sensitive to the anxieties of local communities regarding discharge of patients. Thus, while families and the police used the state hospital as a "last resort" for dealing with troubled individuals, the individuals who had been a problem for the outside community became a problem for the hospital. State hospitals accumulated large numbers of very disturbed, psychotic, long-stay patients. Treatments during these years were limited and experimental. Hospital staff placed hoods on patients' heads in an effort to quiet their minds. Staff gave patients cold baths because of the belief that they calmed the nerves. Physicians applied electroshocks to patients' heads to cure the presumed imbalances. Lobotomies, surgery to cut the nerves from the forebrain to the midbrain, were also attempted and showed the desperation of medicine in dealing with these perplexing illnesses (Gronfein 1985).

The conditions in state hospitals came to public attention after World War II. Mennonites, the Bretheren, and Quakers, given conscientious objector status during the war, worked in state mental hospitals and reported on the deplorable conditions of patients in the hospitals (Sareyan 1994). A 1945 *Life* magazine exposé, "The Shame of the States," revealed graphically the conditions in asylums, and a popular 1948 movie, *The Snake Pit*, dramatized the plight of a woman who finds herself in an insane asylum. The criticisms of asylums continued into the 1960s and 1970s, two decades that witnessed the civil rights and women's movement and societal conflict and opposition to the Vietnam War. These challenges to authority represented a shift in American consciousness manifested in the popular culture. The critique of asylums found expression in Ken Kesey's popular 1962 novel, *One Flew Over the Cuckoo's Nest*, followed by the 1975 movie based on the novel. In the public mind, the state hospital became a symbol of disorder and exclusion.

Academic analysts reinforced the view of the asylum as a repressive and unneeded institution. Chief among these critics was psychiatrist Thomas Szasz, a leader in the antipsychiatry movement. Szasz claimed that mental illness was a myth, a name given for problems in living rather than an illness. He asserted that psychiatry had never proven in any conventional scientific sense that mental illnesses were in fact physical illnesses and, thus, in need of medical treatment. Szasz maintained that what we consider a mental "illness" was a construction of psychiatric authority instead of a product of a diseased mind (Szasz 1961). French philosopher and historian Michel Foucault (1965/1988) similarly asserted that the modern concept of madness was a cultural invention of control, and Scottish psychiatrist R. D. Laing (1960) argued that the schizophrenic patient was often playing at being mad. Sociologist Erving Goffman (1961/1990) based his classic study of asylums on his field work from 1955 to 1957 in St. Elizabeth's, a public mental hospital.

Framing the Need for Deinstitutionalization

While the conditions in state mental hospitals rightfully came under attack, the conditions themselves do not explain deinstitutionalization and the movement to community care. Pressures for change came because of the needs and interests of several groups who were able to "package" or "frame" dein-stitutionalization as serving the freedom, self-determination, autonomy, dignity, and integrity of the mentally ill. These values were in harmony with other social and legal changes occur-ring in the 1960s and 1970s that used the courts and federal legislation as the legal mechanisms to obtain rights. The groups involved in supporting deinstitutionalization included civil lib-ertarians, state fiscal conservatives and the federal government, and the medical establishment.

CIVIL LIBERTARIANS. Groups such as the American Civil Lib-erties Union (ACLU) claimed that the asylum was a repres-sive institution that deprived the mentally ill housed in asylums of their rights. Several court decisions in the 1970s responded to this critique and caused sweeping changes in the involun-tary commitment laws. Three cases are especially noteworthy. In 1976, a federal district court transformed mental health law in the case of *Lessard v. Schmidt* (349 F. Supp. 1078 [E.D. Wis. 1972]). The court struck down Wisconsin's civil commitment law as unconstitutional and set a narrow dangerousness stan-dard for civil commitment: involuntary civil commitment was only permissible when "there is an extreme likelihood that if the person is not confined he will do immediate harm to himself or others." In addition, the court for the first time required that commitment proceedings provide the mentally ill with all the constitutional protections accorded for a criminal suspect. State after state followed Wisconsin in sharply narrowing the grounds for civil confinement. Three years later, in *O'Connor v. Donald-son* (422 U.S. 563 [1975]), the U.S. Supreme Court ruled that a finding of "mental illness" alone cannot justify a state's locking a person up against his will and keeping him indefinitely in custo-dial confinement. A state cannot, the court held, constitutionally confine a nondangerous individual who is capable of surviv-ing safely in freedom. Four years later in *Addington v. Texas* (441

U.S. 418 [1979]), the Supreme Court set the standard for civil commitment. It raised the burden of proof required to commit persons from the usual civil burden of proof of "preponderance of evidence" to "clear and convincing evidence."

STATE FISCAL CONSERVATIVES AND THE FEDERAL GOVERNMENT. Congress insured that the policy of deinstitutionalization would transform the delivery of mental health services by enacting the Community Mental Health Centers Act (Pub. L. No. 88–164 [1963]) along with the Institutionalized Mental Disease (IMD) exclusion (42 U.S.C. §1396d [a] [1994]). The CMHCA provided a massive infusion of federal funds to state agencies that developed small mental health centers within the community. The IMD exclusion was a federal law that forbade federal Medicaid funds for state psychiatric hospitals. Thus, the financial incentive was set for states to empty their state hospitals by relying on community mental health centers largely funded by the federal government. States also wanted to empty their asylums because of their own financial burden. State hospital admissions increased 52 percent between 1955 and 1972, calling for the construction of new hospitals to house the growing numbers of patients. Fiscal conservatives saw the reduction of the inpatient population as an economic necessity (Bassuk and Gerson 1978, 47; Reich and Siegal 1973, 38–39).

Finally, in 1972, through Social Security amendments, the federal government further stimulated state governments to make discharge and early release of the mentally ill their mental health policy. Federal legislation imposed financial penalties on states for not implementing effective programs for controlling unnecessary use of mental hospitals, skilled nursing facilities, and intermediate care facilities, including institutions for the retarded (Rose 1979, 446). Congress also authorized the Supplemental Security Income (SSI) program to begin as a standard program of federal assistance in 1974. Designed to help aged, blind, and disabled individuals who have little or no income, SSI provides cash to meet basic needs for food, clothing, and shelter (42 U.S.C. §§1381–1385f [1972]). Other legislation in 1975 continued to stimulate community-based services, empty state hospitals, and transfer funds from public to private facilities and programs (Rose 1979, 446).

THE MEDICAL ESTABLISHMENT. While the antipsychiatry movement raised questions about the nature of mental illness and its treatment, deinstitutionalization did not result in psychiatry losing control over the definition and treatment of mental illness. Instead, control was now exercised in another setting—the community instead of the state mental hospital. In part, this was possible because of the discovery of psychotropic drugs that could serve an important social control function. In 1954, the Food and Drug Administration approved the use of a new tranquilizing drug, chlorpromazine, marketed under the trade name Thorazine. State mental hospitals were the first to use the drug, and state hospital physicians were genuinely impressed with what they saw when they introduced Thorazine and other new psychotropic drugs in the hospital setting. Once hospitals established the drugs' effectiveness, the pressures toward deinstitutionalization intensified and the medical establishment supported its implementation (Gronfein 1985).

Rose (1979, 42–44) claims that it was possible for the medical profession to maintain control of mental illness because the reigning model of individualism from the broader societal ideology was compatible with medical profession's construction of mental illness. What this means is that in the individualism model of the 1960s and 1970s that emphasized the values of freedom, self-determination, autonomy, dignity, and integrity of the individual placed more emphasis on individuals as internally accountable or responsible for their behavior. In the case of mental illness, the causal relations that the medical profession asserted for diagnosis were only at the individual level—between observed behaviors classified as symptoms and the disease categories that the medical profession created as receptacles of these symptoms. The medical profession, like the larger society, largely ignored the broad social environment that contains explanations of mental illness within dimensions of social life, in particular, the inverse relationship between social class and mental illness (Hudson 2005). Therefore, whether the medical profession considered individual defect in the person as organic or psychological, the dominant medical perspective claimed mental illness as within the province of medical control and designated various methods of treatment for the person. When the economic needs of the state called for the treatment of the mentally ill to move into the community, both the medical establishment and the state government asserted that the basis for change was in fact a response to a therapeutic innovation—psychotropic drugs—and humane considerations—the dignity and liberty of the individual. Lost in this individuated model was the recognition of the complex relationship between the social environment and mental illness.

The Failure of Deinstitutionalization

Evidence soon indicated that deinstitutionalization, from the point of view of community treatment of the mentally ill, was rhetoric rather than reality. It soon became apparent that optimism about deinstitutionalization was shortsighted as federal funding for treatment waxed and waned and community integration proved difficult to enact. What many had forgotten was how state hospitals had provided not only treatment but also a supervised community for the mentally ill (Bachrach 1984). Asylums had effectively prevented the mentally ill from accessing illicit drugs and alcohol and insured that patients consistently received medication. As a system of social control, asylums were able to manage, although often not with the best humanitarian conditions, the social confinement of a large deviant population.

In the community, no longer hidden behind asylum walls, many people with severe mental illnesses—like many ordinary Americans—experimented with illicit drugs and became dependent on alcohol. Unfortunately, many people with severe mental illnesses began to rely on these substances to help with cope with their symptoms and the challenge of living in communities that did not always welcome their presence and saw them as deviants in need of control.

More importantly, scientific research began to clarify a particular manifestation of mental illness that was not fully understood: people with mental illness often did not consider themselves mentally ill. Despite fervent efforts to explain their symptoms, people with severe mental illness like schizophrenia and manic-depression adamantly believe that their symptoms are normal reality (Amador et al. 1994). Whether those symptoms were hallucinations of mysterious voices telling them to harm themselves or delusions in which the mentally ill believed the government was spying on them, no amount of argument, proof, or persuasion can undo the belief. Medications often helped, but when individuals stopped taking them, most also stopped believing that their symptoms are signs of mental illness and instead become lost in their psychosis. Often, the seriously mentally ill believe that those most desperately trying to help them are actually harming them, including their families and doctors.

Additionally, as the deinstitutionalization years progressed, it became clear that while psychotropic medicines like Thorazine were much better than previous therapies, they still fell far short of perfect. Medicine often makes pharmacological interventions based on two qualities: efficacy and tolerability. While drugs like Thorazine possess good efficacy in treating psychotic symptoms, numerous side effects accompany the drugs that patients find intolerable. These include akathisia (an unpleasant sense of inner restlessness), dystonia (involuntary muscle contractions),

FOCUS 2.2. CONDITIONS OF CONFINEMENT:
THE CASE OF TIMOTHY SOUDERS

Scott Pelley, correspondent for the CBS program *60 Minutes,* reported on February 11, 2007, on the case of Timothy Souders, a twenty-one-year-old prisoner at Southern Michigan Correctional Center who suffered from manic depression. Souders was serving a sentence of three to five years for resisting arrest and assault. While in prison, Souders took a shower without permission. His punishment for the shower was placement in solitary confinement. A surveillance camera tape-recorded his stay there. While in solitary, he broke the toilet and flooded his cell. Correctional officers placed him in "top of bed" restraints: he spent four days shackled to a cement slab as punishment; he was restrained for stretches of twelve hours, sixteen hours, and seventeen hours. While shackled, he ate and drank little and did not take any psychotropic medication. A physician saw him once but simply examined the sores on his wrists caused by the restraints. Souders lay in his own waste and had bedsores. At the end of four days, a nurse went to his cell and took vital signs, reporting that he had a "faint pulse." Souders died in his cell. The autopsy found that he died from hypothermia, with dehydration as a contributing factor. At the time of his death, the prison had been operating without on-site psychiatric services for the 1,400 prisoners since May 2006. For more about the Timothy Souders segment on *60 Minutes,* go to http://www.cbsnews.com/stories/2007/02/08/60 minutes/main2448074.shtml.

impotence, and many others. While the addition of secondary medicines can counteract these side effects, these medicines have their own side effects that patients also find intolerable.

THE TRANSCARCERATION OF THE MENTALLY ILL

Now communities had to deal with the deviant behaviors of the mentally ill living outside institutions. During the 1980s, many commentators began to decry the plight of the homeless. Research conducted by social scientists soon revealed the true face of the homeless: they were largely the mentally ill who refused to believe there was anything wrong with their minds, but struggled daily with a host of psychiatric symptoms. Many of homeless were addicted to drugs and alcohol (Torrey 1997). Torrey described a significant dilemma resulting from deinstitutionalization: the "transfer" or "transcarceration" of the mentally ill from asylums to jails and prisons. The control of mentally ill people was being transferred from medical agents to criminal justice agents.

Torrey noted that a number of studies began to document this "transcarceration" of the mentally ill in the mid 1970s. Studies of jails reported a significant number of seriously mentally ill inmates who had formerly been state mental hospital patients (Torrey 1997, 28–29). By the early 1980s, researchers began to examine seriously the problem of mentally ill people in jails. Research by Teplin (1990) and Guy, Platt, Zwerling, and Bullock (1985), for example, found an alarmingly high incidence of serious mental illness such as schizophrenia and mania among jail inmates. A study conducted by the Public Citizen Health Research Group and the National Alliance for the Mentally Ill (Torrey et al. 1992) mailed questionnaires to the directors of all county and city jails in the United States asking them to estimate the percentage of inmates who on any given day "appeared to have a serious mental illness." Forty-one percent of the jail directors replied, representing 62 percent of

FOCUS 2.3: MENTALLY ILL PRISONERS IN THE
GENERAL PRISON POPULATION

A study of New York State prisons by the Correctional
Association of New York described the following examples of mentally ill prisoners confined in a general population cellblock:

- Inmate RB was huddled on the floor of his cell with a
  blanket draped over his head. . . . According to a corrections officer, the inmate had arrived on the block
  two weeks before from Central New York Psychiatric
  Center and had not left the floor of his cell for showers, meals, or recreation since then. Inmates in neigh-
  boring cells said that they gave him food. A deputy
  superintendent . . . stated that mental health staff believed the inmate was trying to "manipulate" his way
  back to the hospital.
- Inmate SP was lying in his bed, stock-still and star-
  ing into space. He appeared dazed and catatonic. He
  either would not or could not speak. A correction officer on the block reported that the inmate had not
  spoken to anyone *in almost a year.* . . .
- Inmate AP had not left his cell for showers or recreation "for several months," according to the correction officer. He sat in his cell picking incessantly at
  his scalp. He seemed disoriented and paranoid. When
  we asked if he wanted to speak with a mental health
  counselor, he refused. (Correctional Association of
  New York 2004, 10)

all jail inmates in the United States. Overall, the jail directors estimated that 7.2 percent of inmates appeared to have a serious mental illness.

Studies of prison inmates also found a disproportionate percentage of severely mentally ill individuals (Torrey 1997, 30–31). The American Psychiatric Association reported research estimating that perhaps as many as one in five prisoners were seriously mentally ill (American Psychiatric Association 2000, xix). As mentioned in chapter 1, a Department of Justice study (Ditton 1999) reported that roughly 16 percent of prison and jail inmates had some form of mental illness, and a later study by the Department of Justice (James and Glaze 2006) reported that at midyear 2005 more than half of all prison and jail inmates had a mental health problem. The study defined mental health problem as follows: a recent history or symptoms of a mental health problem that must have occurred in the twelve months prior to the interview, including a clinical diagnosis or treatment by a mental health professional. The study used symptoms of mental disorders as specified in the *Diagnostic and Statistical Manual of Mental Disorders* (*DSM-IV*). Based on these criteria, the report noted the following: about 24 percent of state prisoners, 14 percent of federal prisoners, and 21 percent of jail inmates reported a recent history of a mental health problem. More than two-fifths of state prisoners (43 percent) and more than half of jail inmates (53 percent) met the criteria for mania. About 23 percent of state prisoners and 30 percent of jail inmates reported symptoms of major depression. An estimated 15 percent of state prisoners and 24 percent of jail inmates reported symptoms that met the criteria for a psychotic disorder.

These statistics demonstrate that, to a significant extent, we have adopted the apparatus of the criminal justice system to monitor and control the mentally ill. In the absence of asylums, unsupervised mentally ill deviants who are not in treatment in their communities find themselves at high risk for intervention by the criminal justice system. Incarceration results because mentally ill individuals who are not receiving treatment may commit crimes. In sum, mental illness is a risk factor, and we primarily use the criminal justice system as the method to control this kind of deviant behavior. Public safety, individual accountability, and punishment dominate the values of American society, and placing the seriously mentally ill in prisons serves to further those values. The use of the correctional system to house the mentally ill documents the social meaning of mental illness as moral failure deserving punishment by incarceration.

Conditions of Confinement

Federal and state correctional systems confine prisoners who are mentally ill to the same facilities as other prisoners unless there is a transfer to acute care or a hospital setting (Beck and Maruschak 2001, 4). Research indicates that prisons and jails are not equipped to treat or understand the behaviors of the incarcerated mentally ill; however, the only constitutional protection for prisoners is the Eighth Amendment's prohibition against "cruel and unusual punishments." Other approaches to protecting the rights of the incarcerated mentally ill include federal legislation. The U.S. Department of Justice can investigate the treatment of mentally ill prisoners under the Civil Rights of Institutionalized Persons Act (42 U.S.C. §1997–1997j [2006]). Under CRIPA, the Justice Department has secured agreements at federal, state, and local levels for improvements in the conditions of confinement for mentally ill prisoners. However, in the past five years, CRIPA has investigated few cases. Prisoners have brought most of the suits initiated to address the treatment of those incarcerated with serious mental illness (Human Rights Watch 2003, 209–14).

Investigations and lawsuits concerning the conditions of confinement of mentally ill prisoners document the reliance on punishment as the primary response and the paucity of mental health treatment. The American Psychiatric Association (2000, 4) concluded that prison access to mental health treatment is impeded by delays in transmitting prisoners' oral or written requests for care, permitting unreasonable delays before patients are seen by mental health staff or outside consultants, and the imposition of fees that prevent or deter prisoners from seeking care. The lack of treatment creates a climate in which mentally ill inmates may repeatedly violate the rules of the prison because of their mental disorder; however, correctional officers view their actions as volitional and consequently hold inmates responsible for their behavior. According to the Bureau of Justice Statistics (cited in Ditton 1999), mentally ill prisoners in state and federal prisons as well as local jails are more likely to have been involved in a fight with other prisoners, and correctional officers are more likely to charge them with breaking prison rules. Moreover, correctional officers often lack training about mental illness and frequently believe that mentally ill behaviors reflect manipulation or malingering (Human Rights Watch 2003, 106–9).

In addition to these problems, other prisoners may victimize mentally ill inmates. Mentally ill prisoners are vulnerable to assault, sexual abuse, exploitation, and extortion. The Correctional Association of New York (2004, 5) found that 54 percent of prisoners in New York's intermediate care units for mentally ill prisoners reported victimization in the general population, including having property stolen and physical and/or sexual assaults. Fifty-seven percent reported not feeling safe in the general population. Other prisoners may share the fears, misconceptions, and erroneous beliefs about mental illness that exist among corrections officers and in the larger society leading to unwillingness to associate with inmates who have mental illness.

While the mentally ill face numerous issues when incarcerated, three issues especially illustrate the dilemmas created when we use prisons and jails to house them: (1) excessive use of force by corrections officers, (2) segregation and isolation, and (3) self-mutilation and suicide.

EXCESSIVE USE OF FORCE. Research indicates that correctional officers often act more aggressively than they should to restrain mentally ill prisoners because they do not know how to react to the often irrational and sometimes violent behavior of mentally ill prisoners. Mentally ill prisoners involved in altercations with correctional officers are often restrained and sometimes seriously injured or killed. The cause of death is frequently positional asphyxiation, which occurs when correctional officers place the prisoner in a prone position with the prisoner's arms behind his back, making it impossible for the respiratory muscles to work properly. The inability to breathe is aggravated and a fatal outcome more likely when one or more officers kneel, sit, or stand on the prisoner (Human Rights Watch 2003, 80–81). Several mentally ill prisoners have died in recent years after placement in restraining chairs. Human Rights Watch reported the following examples:

> In 1997, Michael Valent, a mentally ill prisoner in Utah, died when he developed blood clots after spending sixteen hours strapped nude in a restraining chair.

> In 1997, a mentally ill man in a jail in Osceola County, Florida, died after being placed in a restraining chair and having his head snapped back so violently that he suffered fatal injuries to his brain stem.

> In a jail in Jacksonville, Florida, in 1999, a twenty-year-old mentally ill man died reportedly after guards choked him while he was in a restraining chair. (2003, 82)

SEGREGATION AND ISOLATION. Since the mid-1980s, corrections departments have increasingly chosen to segregate mentally ill prisoners into solitary confinement cells, or special housing units (SHUs). Corrections departments use these cells to segregate prisoners temporarily for breaking prison rules. In SHUs, prisoners typically spend twenty-three out of twenty-four hours locked alone in 14' x 8', sometimes windowless cells. Prisoners eat in their cells and can only leave for showers and solitary exercise, in an empty 9' x 7' caged balcony, a few times per week (Human Rights Watch 2003, 141–47). In 2004, the Correctional Association of New York reported that 23 percent of all prisoners in SHUs are on the mental health caseload. According to its survey of a sample of prisoners in New York State's SHUs, nearly one-third of the SHU prisoners on the mental health caseload have had prior psychiatric hospitalizations. Over one-half suffer from depression; 28 percent have diagnoses of either schizophrenia or bipolar disorder. The study also found that the average SHU sentence for mentally ill prisoners is six times longer than that reported for SHU prisoners generally (Correctional Association of New York 2004, 11–12).

Mental health experts believe that prolonged confinement in conditions of isolation, idleness, and reduced mental stimulation is psychologically destructive to individuals, and especially so to the mentally ill. Moreover, across the country, there is insufficient staff to attend to the high proportion of mentally ill prisoners in segregation. Many are untreated or undertreated because of the belief among staff that mentally ill inmates manipulate their symptoms to get out of segregation (Human Rights Watch 2003, 154–60).

SELF-MUTILATION AND SUICIDE. Mental illness is a high risk factor for self-mutilation and suicide. In their detailed analysis of mental illness in U.S. prisons, Human Rights Watch documented the kinds of self-mutilation by mentally ill prisoners. Included is a description by Elaine Lord, superintendent at the Bedford Hill Correctional Facility in New York, concerning self-mutilation by women prisoners. They self-mutilate by "cutting their own throat, legs, arms, or wrist; head banging, inserting foreign objects under the skin or into wounds or surgical sites on the body; overdosing on medication; or swallowing an extraordinary variety of objects including, but not limited to, knitting needles, screws, straight pins, safety pins, pens, pencils, light bulbs, springs, nails, pieces of radiator, uniform name tags, pieces of wall, and chips of paint" (Human Rights Watch 2003, 14). Examples in other correctional institutions point to the perception by corrections that self-mutilation is an act by manipulative prisoners seeking attention rather than an indication of a genuine mental health problem. Lawsuits filed against correctional institutions allege abuse and neglect of seriously mentally ill prisoners. In particular, Human Rights Watch reported a lawsuit filed against the Georgia Department of Corrections in March 2002 that included the following example of self-mutilation: "In the summer of 2001, a third prisoner 'died during a "cutting party"'—when several prisoners on a cell block begin cutting themselves in tandem—after being placed in a cell with a knife blade left in it. The prisoner 'cut himself so severely that he bled to death'" (Human Rights Watch 2003, 178).

In 2005, the Bureau of Justice Statistics (Mumola 2005) reported a sharp decline in suicide and homicide in state prisons and local jails during the period from 1983 to 2002; however, the report did not include the prior mental health history of inmates as a variable for analysis. In 2002, New York's Office of Mental Health, which provides mental health services to New York prisoners, reported that 70 percent of prisoners who committed suicide had a history of mental illness. Forty percent of them had received a mental health service within three days of the suicide and 40 percent had prior stays in psychiatric hospitals. Forty percent of inmates with mental illness reported acts of self-harm during their current incarceration.

Efforts at self-harm are particularly prevalent in segregated, high-security settings (Human Rights Watch 2003, 179–81). In New York State prisons from 1998 to April 2004, 34 percent of

---

Focus 2.4. The "Balloon Theory" of
Social Control of the Mentally Ill

The idea that we alternately use asylums and prisons to serve as the social control agents for the mentally ill is not a "new" policy born of the 1960s. E. Fuller Torrey reports that Lionel Penrose studied the relationship between mental disease and crime in European countries and demonstrated an inverse correlation between prison and psychiatric hospital populations. As one rose, the other fell. Known as the balloon theory—push in one part of a balloon, and another part will bulge out—George Palermo and his colleagues published in 1991 an extensive analysis hypothesizing the balloon theory using data on U.S. mental hospitals, jails, and prisons for the eighty-three years between 1904 and 1987. They found the theory valid, concluding that "the number of the mentally ill in American jails and prisons supports the thesis of progressive transinstitutionalization. . . . jails have become a repository of pseudo offenders—the mentally ill" (Torrey 1997).

---

the system's seventy-six suicides occurred in disciplinary lockdown, although inmates in these units comprised 7 percent of the total prison population. The Department of Corrections in New York States, similar to correction systems in other states, issues misbehavior reports to inmates who mutilate or attempt to kill themselves (Correctional Association of New York 2004, 5–6).

REACTION TO DEINSTITUTIONALIZATION:
OUTPATIENT COMMITMENT TREATMENT

While transcarceration of the mentally ill from asylum to prisons was occurring, the *Goldstein* case, and others like it, generated a great deal of publicity and public concern about mentally ill individuals who live unsupervised in the community and may need medication. In response to *Goldstein*, New York State created the Assisted Outpatient Treatment Program (AOT), also know as "Kendra's Law" in 1999 (Assisted Outpatient Treatment, N.Y. Ment. Hyg. L.§9.60 [2007]). AOT provides for outpatient treatment for certain people with mental illnesses that, in view of their treatment history and present circumstances, are unlikely to survive safely in the community without supervision. The law establishes a procedure for obtaining court orders for individuals with mental illnesses to receive and accept outpatient treatment. The legislation also establishes a procedure for admission to an inpatient setting in cases where the patient fails to comply with the ordered treatment and poses a risk of harm to self or others. While outpatient programs like Kendra's Law focus on mandated treatment, which often includes counseling and session with a psychiatrist, most programs lack the legal authority to medicate patients against their will. Thus there are real limits associated with outpatient commitment despite its acclaimed ability to solve the outpatient mental health crisis.

Although outpatient assistance treatment like New York State's AOT existed in some states since the 1970s, it was not until the late 1990s that it moved to center stage in the mental health arena. Deinstitutionalization and fragmented outpatient resources created the impetus for increased reliance on outpatient commitment programs (Torrey 2001; Zanni and de Veau 1986). The notion behind these treatment programs appeared simple: preserve patient liberties by allowing for a least restrictive environment to monitor treatment compliance while acknowledging that many seriously mentally ill individuals need an element of coercive care to maintain such compliance. Nationwide, over twenty-three states have adopted AOT programs with varying degrees of success.

Outpatient commitment treatment is not without controversy. Supporters of outpatient commitment point to the "revolving-door" phenomenon in which many seriously mentally ill individuals lead lives that cycle through repeated hospitalizations, poor self-care, and substance abuse (Scheid-Cook 1991; Hiday and Scheid-Cook 1987; Torrey 1997). They cite the fact that a hallmark of many serious mental disorders is the patient's lack of insight into their own illness as a major factor in this pattern (Torrey 2001). Homelessness, poverty, and poor support systems often intensify stress beyond the abilities of mentally ill individuals to cope effectively and maintain adequate treatment compliance (Fischer and Breakey 1986; Kress 2000).

Critics argue that outpatient commitment is an inherently coercive program that uses the threat of a court order to force patients to accept intrusive treatment plans that allow for extensive monitoring of patient's progress (Hoge and Grottole 2000). Critics also argue that outpatient commitment focuses on negative stereotypes, often depicting mentally ill individuals as inherently violent, irresponsible, and unpredictable (Allen and Smith 2001; Hoge and Grottole 2000; Slobogin 1994). Moreover, they argue that outpatient commitment sends a double message, one that presents liberation and collaboration to the patient while also promising mandated treatment and public safety to family members and society (Hoge and Grottole 2000; Hughes 2001). Critics state that if we funded traditional outpatient services, outpatient commitment would be unnecessary since many severely mentally ill individuals live in poverty and do not have access to private mental health care, and thus often wait in need of care (Hoge and Grottole 2000).

There is an additional element of ethical concern with outpatient commitment. Many patients are not fully aware of their legal rights nor do they understand the legal parameters of the outpatient commitment laws themselves. Borum et al. (1999) interviewed a sample of over 300 people awaiting an AOT hearing. Ninety percent of the respondents believed that out-patient commitment required them to take medication with-out the benefit of any additional legal proceeding even though under most current statutes that is not the case. A further area of concern is whether current research methods are adequate to properly survey the effectiveness of AOT. Draine (1997) points to the fact that most studies only measure recidivism, violence, and noncompliance. This seems to confirm critics' assessments that outpatient commitment laws are more concerned with public fear and safety than with treatment effectiveness. Sup-porters, however, suggest that these are appropriate outcome measures since outpatient commitment is reserved for those patients with demonstrable histories of criminal justice involve-ment and treatment nonadherence.

CONCLUSION: DEINSTITUTIONALIZATION AND CONTINUITY OF CONFINEMENT

In this chapter, we have examined the change in the social reaction to mental illness that reflects the dominance of a puni-tive paradigm toward the mentally ill rather than a treatment paradigm. Harcourt (2006) sees the issue as a "continuity of con-finement" rather than some type of transformative shift. Draw-ing on the work of social theorists of the 1960s who examined asylums, Harcourt claims that there is "a continuity of spatial exclusion and confinement between the asylum and the peni-tentiary" (Harcourt 2006, 1781). Like Goffman's (1961/1990) research on asylums and Foucault's (1961/1988) investigation of madness, Harcourt places asylums within the same kind of exclusionary space as prisons, sanitariums, orphanages, boarding schools, and monasteries. Harcourt agrees with the analysis of Rothman, who claimed that these total institutions are places of "first resort, the preferred solution to the problems of poverty, crime, delinquency, and insanity" (Rothman 1971, 131). Society uses these institutions because of the perceived need to restore social balance during a time of instability. Harcourt notes that the social theorists of the 1960s and 1970s portrayed the mental hospital as an inherently repressive institution, not very different from the prison.

What are we to make of these social theorists and Harcourt's claim in light of deinstitutionalization? The argument is that there is a continuity of confinement because prisons, mental institutions, and other total institutions are used to house social deviants that society finds unacceptable. The transfer from asylums to prisons is not a new phenomenon (see Focus 2.4). It represents a method of social control for dealing with particular social problems at a particular point in time. The question, Harcourt says, is not how many people with mental illness are in the criminal justice system. Rather, the question should be whether the criminal justice system caught in its wider net the type of people at the margin of society—the class of deviants from predominant social norms—who used to be caught up in the asylum and mental hospital (Harcourt 2006). The issue for us to understand is why we have chosen the prison rather than the mental hospital. The conflict between the assumptions of criminal law and the behavioral sciences can provide some answers and forms the remaining chapters of the book.

CHAPTER 3

Competency to Stand Trial and Competency to Be Executed

Let me make this clear, please: This trial, the bad memory, it's a nuisance to me. I want to have as little to do with these proceedings as possible.

—Ralph J. Tortorici[*]

ON THE MORNING of December 14, 1994, Ralph Tortorici stormed into a lecture hall at the State University of New York (SUNY) at Albany campus. Dressed in military fatigues and armed with a semi-automatic rifle, eighty rounds of ammunition, and a hunting knife, he took hostage a group of students. After yelling "Stop government experimentation," Tortorici demanded to see both the governor of New York State and the president of the SUNY educational system. He threatened to kill his hostages and fired the rifle at a projection screen. After a two-hour standoff, several of the students overpowered him. During the struggle, Tortorici stabbed one student and shot another student in the scrotum.

---

[*]Statements made in open court by Ralph Tortorici before the judge presiding at his trial (*People v. Tortorici,* 709 N.E. 2d 87, 91 [N.Y. 1999]).

Shortly after his arraignment the next day, two psychiatric examiners found Tortorici incompetent to stand trial: they found him unable to understand the charges against him and to assist in his own defense. Following standard procedure, the court remanded him to Mid-Hudson Psychiatric Center, a secure forensic hospital, for observation and treatment. Upon admission, Tortorici displayed the symptoms of paranoid schizophrenia. Notes indicated that he was delusional and psychotic with paranoid beliefs (Mid-Hudson Psychiatric Center 1995). While hospitalized, he refused all medication but he received counseling. On March 20, 1995, after ten weeks as an inpatient, hospital psychiatrists judged Tortorici competent to stand trial and returned him to Albany.

From that date until the start of jury selection some ten months later, Ralph Tortorici awaited trial in the Albany County Jail, receiving no medication or further psychological treatment. During a pretrial hearing on November 16, 1995, his attorney told the judge that Tortorici no longer wished to be present during the pretrial proceedings or the actual trial. Given the unusual request, the judge asked him to appear in court on several occasions, each time speaking briefly to him. At one pretrial hearing, the judge questioned him about his request, and Tortorici stated, "I speak English, Judge. I don't desire to be present. I made that point clear. That is all ... I do not desire to be present. No further comments" (*People v. Tortorici*, 709 N.E. 2d 87, 91 [N.Y. 1999]). On January 3, 1996, at the beginning of jury selection, defense counsel again informed the court that Tortorici wished to waive his right to be present during the entire trial proceedings. The judge questioned him again, and he replied, "Let me make this clear, please. This trial, the bad memory, it's a nuisance to me. I want to have as little to do with these proceedings as possible" (*People v. Tortorici*).

Since Tortorici was claiming that he was not guilty by reason of insanity, the prosecution was entitled to have him examined

FOCUS 3.1. RALPH TORTORICI AND
A CRIME OF INSANITY

Ralph Tortorici's case generated a great deal of controversy because individuals believed that not only the verdict but the trial itself represented an injustice, especially given Tortorici's suicide in prison. The primary concern raised was the failure to order a new competency hearing given the forensic report by Dr. Lawrence Siegel and Ralph Tortorici's extremely unusual request to be absent from the trial proceedings. More specifically at issue was the failure of the judge to order a hearing. New York State Criminal Procedure Law, section 730.30 (2006), concerning fitness to proceed at trial requires that a judge "must issue" an order of examination when the court believes that the defendant may be an incapacitated person. The failure of the judge to order such a hearing for Tortorici was the major issue heard and decided by the appeals courts who, unfortunately, found that the judge did not abuse his discretion.

PBS Frontline produced a documentary, *A Crime of Insanity*, to describe the controversy generated by the case. The documentary presented the reflections of key players in the case: forensic examiner Siegel, prosecutor Cheryl Coleman, chief assistant district attorney Larry Wiest, defense attorney Peter Lynch, trial judge Larry Rosen, and family members of Tortorici. Perhaps the most poignant and revealing interview was the interview with prosecutor Coleman concerning her changed view of the case and her role in it. Shortly after Tortorici's suicide, she resigned her position an assistant district attorney. In discussing her involvement with the case, Coleman revealed that she felt responsible for Tortorici's death because of her win-at-any-cost approach. She said, "When you're a trial lawyer, it doesn't even matter what side you're on, because you go into a zone and you're into the battle. You're not even really thinking about right, you're not thinking about wrong. You're not thinking about what your role is supposed to be. You're just thinking about winning, and you're just thinking about doing anything that you have to do, short of lie, cheat, and steal. But you're doing everything that they said you can do to win. That's what we were doing." Later in the interview, she said, "I think I was ashamed that morality and what's right, as opposed to what's legal, plays so little a role in the system, and plays so little a role in what we do, that if that hadn't happened, it might have gone on just never giving a thought to what we do. It was [a] life-altering experience" (http://www.pbs.org/wgbh/pages/frontline/shows/crime/interviews/coleman.html).

For more about *A Crime of Insanity,* see http://www.pbs.org/wgbh/pages/frontline/shows/crime/interviews/.

by an expert of their choice. Dr. Lawrence Siegel, a forensic psychiatrist, examined Tortorici in the presence of defense counsel and prosecution and reported that he was unable to assess Tortorici's mental state at the time of the offense, but that Tortorici was "incapable of rational participation in court proceedings" and "not fit to proceed to trial" (Siegel 1996, 8). Siegel wrote that while Tortorici knew the charges against him, the date and place of the alleged offense, the name of his attorney, and the roles of the major participants in the trial, he was also convinced that there were external governmental forces influencing these persons through waves (Siegel 1996, 8).

The following day, the judge brought this report to the attention of the prosecutor and Tortorici's lawyer. However, although defense counsel acknowledged that Tortorici was suffering from paranoid schizophrenia, counsel stated that he was ready to proceed with the trial. The prosecutor also advised the court that the defendant appeared fit to proceed to trial. Hearing no objections from either the defense or prosecution, the judge, relying upon his own brief observations of Tortorici, and the now eight-month-old report from Mid-Hudson Psychiatric Center, decided that there was no need for the court to order an additional competency evaluation or hearing; instead, the trial proceeded.

Both lay and expert witnesses testified for the defense about how psychotic Ralph Tortorici had been for several years prior to the shootings as well as at the time of his classroom siege at SUNY at Albany. The prosecution argued that while Tortorici was mentally ill, he did not meet the stringent legal definition of insanity. That standard requires that a defendant prove that he did not know either the consequences of his acts or that his conduct was wrong. On February 16, 1996, after deliberating for just one hour, the jury rejected Tortorici's insanity plea and convicted Tortorici of all charges. The judge sentenced him to the maximum term of incarceration allowed under New York State law—a prison term of twenty to forty-seven years. Tortorici appealed his conviction, claiming, in part, that in light of Siegel's report, the judge erred in not ordering a competency hearing. The first court to hear his appeal affirmed his conviction by a vote of 3 to 2 (*People v. Tortorici,* 249 A.D. 2d 588 [App. Div. 1998]). The second court, the Court of Appeals, New York's highest court, also affirmed the conviction by a 5 to 1 margin (*People v. Tortorici,* 709 N.E. 2d 87, 91 [N.Y. 1999]).

After his sentencing, corrections officials placed Ralph Tortorici with the general prison population, but he occasionally spent time in a special prison unit for the severely mentally ill. In August 1999, Tortorici committed suicide by hanging himself from a bed sheet tied to a shelf in his cell.

The Issue of the Defendant's Competence in Criminal Proceedings

The *Tortorici* case illustrates the tension between criminal law and behavioral science concerning the defendant's competence to stand trial (also known as adjudicative competence). This principle, derived from both common law and the Constitution, permits the delay of criminal proceedings for defendants who are unable to take part in their defense because of a mental or physical disorder or mental retardation. Unlike the insanity defense, which is concerned with the defendant's mental capacity at the time of the alleged offense, competency issues may arise at any time during a criminal proceeding and do not involve issues of guilt or innocence.

Although competence to stand trial frequently concerns the "mental state" of the defendant, it is a legal, not clinical decision. A judge rules on the issue of the defendant's fitness to proceed at trial. However, determining whether a court should hospitalize or subject the defendant to a trial depends heavily on clinical opinion. Courts often order competency evaluations at the outset of a criminal prosecution, upon arrest of the defendant, when it appears that the defendant may suffer from a serious mental illness. After a court decides to have a competency evaluation, one or more mental health professionals will examine the defendant and then submit a written report or reports to the court, followed by a formal hearing on the issue of the defendant's competence to stand trial. However, as the *Tortorici* case illustrates, a defendant's competency may wax and wane, especially if there is a long time between a determination that the defendant is competent and the onset of trial proceedings or if the defendant receives no treatment while incarcerated.

FOCUS 3.2. BLACKSTONE ON INCOMPETENCE
TO STAND TRIAL

Writing in the eighteenth century, Sir William Blackstone described the effect on criminal proceedings of a
defendant's incompetence the following way: "If a man
in his sound memory commits a capital offence, and
before arraignment for it, he becomes mad, he ought not
be arraigned for it; because he is not able to plead to it
with that advice and caution that he ought. And if, after
he has pleaded, the prisoner becomes mad, he shall not
be tried; for how can he make his defence?" (Blackstone
1769/1979, 24).

Therefore, the determination of competence to stand trial is a
complex issue that often finds criminal law and the behavioral
sciences with opposing viewpoints concerning how to decide a
defendant's competence to stand trial.

This chapter first examines why competence to stand trial is
an important legal principle in criminal proceedings and looks
at the sources of conflict between criminal law and behavioral
science concerning this principle. We will consider these issues
by reviewing the legal origins of the principle of competency
and the significant U.S. Supreme Court decisions that address
the standard for competency to stand trial and the role of the
judge in competency proceedings. In contrast to the legal perspective, the research of behavioral scientists leads many to
maintain that the Supreme Court standards concerning competence to stand trial are not adequate given the complexities
of criminal proceedings. The second part of the chapter examines the consequences of a finding of incompetence in terms of
two controversial issues: the use of forced medication to restore

competency and the execution of incompetent inmates. These issues highlight the controversies concerning how the legal system should respond to mentally ill defendants.

As we discuss these issues, consider the *Tortorici* case in light of the perspectives of criminal law and the behavioral sciences regarding the criteria for competency to stand trial and the role of behavioral science experts in that determination. One of the issues raised by the case is whether the procedures used and the decision reached served the interests of justice.

COMPETENCE TO STAND TRIAL AND CRIMINAL PROCEEDINGS

The fundamental constitutional principle behind competence to stand trial is that a defendant has a right to be present *mentally* as well as physically during the *entire* criminal proceeding in order to receive a fair trial. When a defendant is confused mentally and therefore unable to understand the legal process or aid in the defense, to continue with the trial would be as unfair as if the person were not there. The Sixth Amendment of the U.S. Constitution, applied to the states though the due process clause of the Fourteenth Amendment, guarantees that defendants must receive a fair trial: it violates due process to convict incompetent defendants. Indeed, the U.S. Supreme Court has ruled that the prohibition against conducting a criminal trial of an incompetent defendant "is fundamental to an adversary system of justice" (*Drope v. Missouri*, 420 U.S. 162 [1975]). Since the accused will bear the punishment if convicted, he or she should have a fundamental understanding of the legal proceeding and be able to assist his or her lawyer. This includes the knowledge that the prosecutor's duty is to try to convict the defendant, the judge presides over the process to ensure fairness, the jury will determine guilt, and the defense attorney's job is to protect and defend the defendant against the accusations.

Common Law Origins

As with the development of the ideas of free will, *mens rea,* and *actus reus* discussed in chapter 1, the principle of competency in criminal proceedings finds its origin in common law's ideas about religion and evil. Researchers have traced its development from the fourteenth century. Courts would permit the criminal trial of a defendant only after the accused entered a plea of "guilty" or "not guilty" to the charges. When a defendant "stood mute" rather than answering to the charges, the court did not move forward with trial but rather undertook an investigation to determine if the defendant was "mute by visitation of God" or "mute of malice." A finding of "mute by visitation of God" referred to defendants who were deaf, mute, or insane. The court excused these defendants from trial. A finding of "mute by malice" meant the courts believed the defendants were capable of understanding the charges but wanted to avoid trial. In medieval times, courts compelled these defendants to enter a plea by several unpleasant methods. Often, courts used a technique known as *peine forte et dure,* which called for the placement of increasingly heavy weights on the defendant's chest until he entered a plea. Other methods included starvation or confinement in a small cell (Poythress et al. 2002, 39).

In the seventeenth century, as the concept of *mens rea* ("guilty mind") was taking hold in criminal law, the conception of competence to stand trial matured to resemble modern standards. Common law courts began to focus on the capability of defendants to participate in their defense and to understand the pending criminal charges. In special competency hearings, twelve-man juries assessed the competency of defendants based on the evidence of the defendant's medical history, military and social background, behavior and appearance at trial, and testimony from lay and professional witnesses who knew or had observed the defendant. Courts incarcerated defendants found incompetent until they became fit to proceed to trial, while defendants found competent proceeded to trial (Appelbaum and Gutheil 2006, 121).

The U.S. Supreme Court and Competence to Stand Trial

Drawing from its common law origins, the concept of competence to stand trial has long been a fixture in criminal law in the United States. However, what exactly constitutes an incompetent defendant is not always clear. Decisions of the Supreme Court have only added to this confusion. In *Dusky v. United States* (362 U.S. 402 [1960]), the Supreme Court articulated a standard for competence to stand trial as a defendant having "sufficient present ability to consult with a lawyer with a reasonable degree of rational understanding" and having a "rational as well as factual understanding of the proceedings against him" (*Dusky v. United States,* 402). According to the *Dusky* decision, judges may not find competence to stand trial simply because the defendant is oriented to time and place and has some recollection of events. Rather, the court emphasized the fact that the defendant must have a reasonable, *present* rational capacity to participate actively in the defense process.

The *Dusky* opinion differs substantially from many of the rulings handed down by the high court in criminal law cases because the entire opinion is less than a half-page long and because, critics argued, the court failed to provide a clear rule that courts could implement in their day-to-day operations. For example, what is "sufficient present ability"? How does one evaluate a defendant's "rational as well as factual understanding of the proceedings against him"? Is a basic understanding of the legal proceedings, as articulated in the common law standard, sufficient to establish competence to stand trial?

The Supreme Court revisited the issue of competency almost six years later in *Pate v. Robinson* (383 U.S. 375 [1966]). Here the issue was whether the judge should have ordered a competency hearing to rule on the evidence concerning the defendant's competence to stand trial. This case concerned a defendant who had a long history of disturbed behavior and a diagnosis of schizophrenia. The defendant claimed that he was insane at the time of the shooting and at the time of his trial, but the trial court did not hold a hearing regarding his mental state at the time of trial. The jury convicted him of murdering his wife. The defendant appealed his conviction, arguing that the trial court violated his constitutional rights when the trial judge did not order a competency hearing. Justice Clark, writing the opinion for the majority, stated that a criminal defendant's Sixth Amendment right to a fair trial requires that the court hold a competency hearing when there is a "bona fide doubt" as to the defendant's present competency. Moreover, Justice Clark's opinion stated that while a defendant's "demeanor at trial might be relevant to the ultimate decision as to his sanity, it cannot be relied upon to dispense with a hearing on that very issue" (*Pate v. Robinson*, 386).

Nine years after *Pate v. Robinson*, a unanimous court in *Drope v. Missouri* (420 U.S. 162 [1975]) attempted to clarify the *Dusky* test and the duty of trial judges to safeguard incompetent defendants from trial proceedings. In *Drope*, the court held that trial judges should not merely serve as passive decision-makers regarding competency issues. Rather, the trial court should exercise an active role in determining a defendant's competence to stand trial and consider a defendant's history of mental illness a significant factor in making its determination. In *Drope*, as in the *Tortorici* trial, the defendant was absent from the proceedings. The court held that the defendant's absence prevented the trial court from having the opportunity "to gauge from his demeanor whether he was able to cooperate with his attorney and to understand the nature and object of the proceedings against him" (*Pate v. Robinson*, 181).

The Behavioral Science Perspective on Competency

Despite the standard for competency articulated by the court, only a handful of states have enacted statutes for competence to

stand trial that specifically mention the words "rational understanding." This is because the decisions just reviewed concerned
federal cases; the court did not specifically articulate a standard
that state courts must follow. Most state laws specifying the standard for an incompetent defendant simply state that the defendant lacks an ability or capacity to understand the nature of
the proceedings and assist in his or her defense. In the *Tortorici*
case, the prosecutor, Cheryl Coleman, said in her 2001 interview on PBS's *Frontline*, "Somebody described competent once
as knowing the difference between a judge and a grapefruit."
Coleman meant to indicate that the standard for competence
to stand trial is a very low one, one in which rational understanding is usually not given emphasis. Yet a lack of rational
understanding was the issue in the *Tortorici* case. Ralph Tortorici
certainly knew that he was on trial and he could describe what
the role of the judge, prosecutor, and defense counsel. However,
as Dr. Siegel's report indicated:

> Much of Mr. Tortorici's communication regarding his legal
> situation makes sense. He is aware of the names of the charges
> against him and has an understanding of what he is alleged
> to have done. However, many of his ideas concerning how
> he should deal with his legal situation, and how others might
> perceive his ideas, betrays his problems with his thinking. His
> thought that persons in the court are influenced through "air
> waves" and "power waves," interferes with his capacity to
> understand the true nature of the proceedings. . . . His abili-
> ties to perceive, recall and relate are variably impaired. His
> perceptions are filtered by his psychotic beliefs. For instance
> he perceives that the examiner has moved in a manner that
> proves the examiner has been subjected to power waves. He
> appears to be able to recall, but much of his recollections
> are of psychotic material. His ability to relate is impaired by
> difficulty expressing himself in a rational manner. While he

is capable of forming a relationship with his attorney (and appears to have formed one), his delusional system is such that there cannot be a joint understanding of the meaning of the trial currently going on. He does seem able to consider advice given to him by his attorney. (Siegel 1996, 8–9)

The lack of emphasis on "rational understanding" in the wording of competency statutes illustrates the differing paradigms with which the two disciplines, law and psychiatry/psychology, often take on issues of competency and sanity. From a mental health perspective, forensic experts frequently determine competence to stand trial by the absence or presence of psychosis, while from a legal perspective, an individual may be psychotic but competent to stand trial if he or she possesses enough insight to know the basics about the trial process. From the perspective of criminalization of the mentally ill, one can argue that the legal standard enables a crime-conscious society to justify prosecuting mentally ill individuals. Indeed, the failure of trial courts to order hearings on the issue of competence to stand trial when the defendant has a history of serious mental illness seems to indicate a skeptical attitude about claims of incompetence—an attitude consistent with the skeptical attitudes of the general population about the mental illness claims of defendants.

Competency as a Context-Based Inquiry

The ability to make reasoned decisions regarding making a *particular decision* or performing a *particular kind of task* (Melton et al. 1997; Schopp 2001) is the crucial issue in determining a defendant's competency from a behavioral science point of view. Behavioral science research findings argue against a uniform standard for competency and instead call for an assessment of defendants that is dependent upon the particular capacities needed at a particular stage of the criminal proceedings. In support of their claim, behavioral scientists have developed many competency instruments, and most recently, researchers have focused their efforts to deconstruct competence into specific cognitive abilities that are quantifiable and measurable (Grisso 2003; Zapf and Viljoen 2003; Poythress et al. 2002; Rogers et al. 2001; Nestor, Daggett, and Price 1999).

One work that is frequently cited by scholars and practitioners as support for the proposition that competence is a context-based inquiry is Bonnie's 1992 conceptualization that competency should be evaluated using two separate but related constructs: competency to assist counsel and decisional competency. Under Bonnie's conceptualization, *competency to assist counsel* encompasses all of the requirements that a defendant, at minimum, must possess in order to proceed at trial. In other words, the defendant must (1) understand the charges, the purpose of the criminal process, and the adversary system, especially the role of defense counsel; (2) appreciate his or her situation as a defendant in a criminal prosecution; and (3) recognize and relate pertinent information to counsel concerning the facts of the case. According to Bonnie and following *Dusky* and common law, criminal proceedings should not take place when a defendant is unable to assist defense counsel.

Decisional competency concerns the specific choices defendants must make throughout the adjudicative process. Unlike many decisions made by attorneys, these are choices that only defendants can make: decisions such as whether to plead guilty or whether to waive certain constitutional rights. From Bonnie's perspective, in some situations a defendant may be found competent to assist counsel but not competent to make these weighty decisions. Lack of decisional competency does not necessarily bar criminal proceedings. This is because Bonnie views decisional competency as a context-dependent inquiry. In other words, whether decisional competency is required depends on the particular decisions that a defendant is required to make at that particular stage of the criminal justice process.

Bonnie maintains that defendants who do not seek to waive any constitutional protections are not required to possess decisional competency. However, decisional competency would be relevant, for example, if a suspect who suffers from mental illness wants to waive Miranda rights and confess to a crime. For a valid waiver, a suspect must give a knowing, voluntary, and intelligent waiver. A "knowing" waiver implies suspects understand their rights and speaks to the manner in which they are informed of their rights. An "intelligent" waiver, by contrast, implies that suspects have made a *rational* choice based on some appreciation of the consequences of the decision. Mentally ill suspects may waive Miranda rights in a valid way as long as the illness does not interfere with their cognitive ability to understand these rights.

In addition to the two standards of competency proposed by Bonnie, Brakel (2003) proposes that criminal proceedings should also evaluate the defendant's *level of competency.* In distinguishing *level* from *standard,* Brakel offers the analogy between the criteria that comprise the two-pronged *Dusky* competency test and the different standards of proof in different legal proceedings (beyond a reasonable doubt, clear and convincing evidence, and preponderance of the evidence). Brakel argues that the matter of level is relevant to both prongs of the competency test in the *Dusky* standard—the ability to understand and the ability to assist—as these abilities are relative. Every competency evaluation, Brakel states, implicitly asks how cognitively deficient the accused is (prong number one) and how functionally deficient (prong number two).

One way to consider the level issue is in terms of the legal consensus that the current competency level/standard is low; one does not have to be very competent to proceed to trial. As Cheryl Coleman, the prosecutor in the *Tortorici* case, stated in her interview for *Frontline,* some view competence to stand trial as knowing the difference between a judge and a grapefruit. Brakel argues that criminal law should consider level of competency as a type of case inquiry. Defense counsel should want a defendant asserting the defense of insanity in a trial for murder to proceed to trial with a low level of competency to support the claim of insanity as the defense. A defendant who does not claim insanity on trial for a crime such as identity theft may need a higher level of competence to satisfy the two-prong *Dusky* test because of the intricate factual defense often mounted in those cases. Such a case would require a high level of competence for the defendant to both assist in the legal defense and understand the nature of the legal proceedings.

In sum, behavioral scientists see the competence issue as a complex one that the law should not reduce to one uniform standard. It is a construct amenable to empirical study, and from such research, behavioral scientists have developed forensic instruments that can assess the capacities of the defendant at a particular stage of a criminal proceeding. The level of competency and the distinction between decisional competency and competency to assist counsel are important considerations not only because these distinctions empirically exist but also because they serve to protect the defendant from unfair criminal proceedings.

The Legal Dismissal of the Behavioral Science View of Competency

The Supreme Court had an opportunity to embrace the findings of behavioral science concerning competence in *Godinez v. Moran* (509 U.S. 389 [1993]). The majority opinion chose to reject the behavioral science conceptualization of competency as a context-based inquiry, one that depended on the types of decisions required of defendants or the kinds of cases in which competency is an issue. The case concerned a man (Moran) who allegedly shot and killed three persons and attempted to kill himself. Initially, he pled not guilty to three

counts of first-degree murder. The trial court ordered evaluations of Moran by two psychiatrists, and both concluded he
was competent to stand trial. The state of Nevada announced its
intention to seek the death penalty. Two and a half months after
the psychiatric evaluations, Moran informed the court that he
wished to discharge his attorneys and change his pleas to guilty.
The reason for his request, according to Moran, was to prevent
the presentation of mitigating evidence at his sentencing. The
court accepted the waiver of counsel and guilty pleas. It found
that Moran was "knowingly and intelligently: waiving his right
to the assistance of counsel, and that his guilty pleas were 'freely
and voluntarily given'" (*Godinez v. Moran,* 393). Moran received
the death sentence for the murders. He appealed, claiming that
he had been mentally incompetent to represent himself.

The Supreme Court noted that while it had described the
standard for competence to stand trial in *Dusky,* it had never
expressly articulated a standard for competence to plead guilty
or waive the right to the assistance of counsel. However, the
court determined that the level of competence required for
defendants to waive a constitutional right is no greater than
required to stand trial: a defendant who stands trial will confront strategic choices that entail relinquishment of the same
rights that a defendant relinquishes who pleads guilty. No basis
existed for requiring a higher level of competence for defendants who choose to plead guilty rather than proceed to trial.
Instead, the court reaffirmed the *Dusky* standard—rational and
factual understanding of the proceedings and ability to assist
counsel—as the uniform standard to assess competency. Requiring that a criminal defendant be competent, the court stated,
"has a modest aim: It seeks to ensure that he has the capacity
to understand the proceedings and to assist counsel. While psychiatrists and scholars may find it useful to classify the various
kinds and degrees of competence, and while States are free to
adopt competency standards that are more elaborate than the

FOCUS 3.3. COLIN FERGUSON: COMPETENCY TO
STAND TRIAL AND ASSIST IN ONE'S OWN DEFENSE

On December 7, 1993, Colin Ferguson, a thirty-five-year-old divorced black Jamaican immigrant, boarded a rush-hour commuter train heading home to Long Island from New York City. After two stops, Ferguson pulled out a 9 mm semiautomatic pistol from a bag he was carrying, stood up, and shot at passengers, killing six and wounding nineteen others. Two passengers tackled Ferguson and pinned him to the ground. Although police arrested him at the scene and passengers positively him identified as the shooter, Ferguson claimed that he was not the shooter. An article in the *Chicago Tribune* on December 9, 1993, reported that in Ferguson's pockets, police found numerous handwritten notes listing the "reasons for this," including "Adelphi University's racism, the EEOC's racism, Worker's Compensation racism, NYC Transit Police, NYC Police [and] the racism of Governor Cuomo's staff."

After Ferguson's arraignment and arrest, forensic experts examined Colin Ferguson to evaluate whether he was competent to stand trial. Since they disagreed, the trial judge ordered a competency hearing. At the hearing, he interviewed Ferguson not only to determine whether Ferguson understood the nature of the charges against him and the trial process but also to consider his request that he represent himself at trial. Ferguson made this request because he disagreed with his lawyers' defense strategy, namely that he had been driven to temporary insanity by black rage. The trial judge found that Ferguson was competent to stand trial, and he permitted Ferguson to represent himself.

(continued)

Focus 3.3. (continued)

Ferguson's trial was highly unusual because he cross-examined the police that arrested him and the victims he shot. His position throughout the trial was that he was not the shooter. While he admitted to bringing the gun on the train, he claimed that he fell asleep, and another man grabbed his gun and began firing. The jury convicted Colin Ferguson on February 17, 1995, of murder of the six passengers who died and additional charges against the nineteen that he wounded. He received six consecutive life sentences. After his conviction, he argued in appellate briefs that he had incompetent counsel (himself).

While Ferguson's original defense counsel and other critics claimed that Ferguson was insane at the time of the shootings and was not competent to stand trial or act as his own defense counsel, other legal scholars take the position that Ferguson took actions to represent himself that most lawyers would have approved. For example, during jury selection, he questioned jurors about their racial biases, he did a reasonably good job of examining and cross-examining witnesses, and he did as well as the prosecution in his closing argument (Ewing and McCann 2006, 177–90).

Dusky formulation, the Due Process Clause does not impose these additional requirements" (*Godinez v. Moran,* 402).

Justice Blackmun, in a passionate dissenting opinion, criticized the failure of the majority of the court to use the more complex and empirically valid standard of competence advocated by behavioral scientists. He noted that in the *Godinez v. Moran* case, the defendant Moran, just three months after his suicide attempt, appeared in court seeking to discharge his public defender, waive his right to counsel, and plead guilty to all three charges of capital murder while under the influence of four different psychotropic medications. Such factual issues should alert a trial court about a defendant's competence to waive constitutional rights (*Godinez v. Moran,* 413).

In terms of the legal standard, Blackmun stated that a finding of competence to stand trial establishes only that the defendant is capable of aiding his attorney in making the critical decisions required at trial or in plea negotiations. The reliability or even relevance of such a finding vanishes, he observed, when the basic premise—that counsel will be present—ceases to exist. At that point, the issue no longer is whether the defendant can proceed with an attorney but whether he can proceed alone. Blackmun concluded that the law should not apply the standard for competency in a vacuum divorced from its specific context, for "competency for one purpose does not necessarily translate to competency for another purpose" (*Godinez v. Moran,* 413).

Forced Medication and Competency to Stand Trial

As indicated earlier in this chapter, a criminal defendant must be mentally competent at all stages of the criminal proceedings—from arrest to sentencing. Although criminal courts frequently order competency evaluations, courts find only approximately 30 percent of defendants incompetent to stand trial (Melton et al. 1997). The low percentage of defendants found incompetent by the courts does not mean that there is a great deal of disagreement between forensic evaluators and the courts. On the contrary, estimates of agreement range from 90 to 99 percent (Nicholson and Kugler 1991; Cruise and Rogers 1998; Zapf and Viljoen 2003). The high rate of agreement reflects the forensic evaluator's application of the legal standard of competency to the evaluation at hand. It does not mean that behavioral scientists agree with the legal standard.

When a court makes a finding that a defendant is incompetent to stand trial, the court typically sends a defendant to a state mental hospital to be "restored" to competence. Most defendants found incompetent are typically suffering from some type of delusional disorder such as schizophrenia. Treatment typically involves the administration of psychotropic medications to treat symptoms. However, incompetent defendants may resist the administration of these medications, and one of the constitutional, as well as ethical, questions concerns the forced administration of medication to attempt to restore the competency of the defendant to stand trial.

The Constitutional Issues

The Constitution implies limits to the state's power to coerce treatment of any illness, mental or otherwise. Psychotropic drugs can have serious, dangerous side effects, and individuals have a significant liberty interest in forced administration of treatment. In *Washington v. Harper* (494 U.S. 210 [1990]), the Supreme Court recognized these concerns when it considered a case of a mentally ill incarcerated man (defendant already convicted of a crime) who did not want to be medicated by prison psychiatrists. The court set forth two criteria for making a decision to force an inmate to take drugs. First, the prisoner must be a danger to himself or others; and second, the prisoner is seriously disruptive to his or her environment and the treatment is in his or her "medical interests." Two years later, the court considered the case of involuntarily medicating a mentally ill defendant who was still facing trial but was refusing medication during the trial proceedings. In *Riggins v. Nevada* (504 U.S. 127 [1992]), the trial court refused to allow the defendant to discontinue his medication despite his arguments that its continuation would affect both his demeanor at trail and his ability to assist meaningfully in his defense. However, the Supreme Court held the due process clause prohibits prosecuting officials from administering involuntary doses of antipsychotic medicines for purposes of rendering the accused competent for trial absent any showing by the state that less intrusive means were available to restore his competency and that he was a danger to himself or others. The government had not made either showing in this case.

More recently, in 2003, the court again faced the involuntary medication issue in the case of *Sell v. United States,* 539 U.S. 166 (2003). The case concerned whether the government may forcibly medicate an incompetent pretrial detainee facing felony insurance fraud charges to restore his competency to stand trial. The court's holding in *Sell* was that the government's interest to make the defendant competent to stand trial outweighed the defendant's right to refuse medication if the government could show all the following. First, the state has an essential interest that outweighs the individual's right to be free of medication. Second, there exists no less intrusive way to meet that goal. Third, the government can prove by clear and convincing evidence that the medication is medically appropriate.

The Ethical Issues

Critics of competency through forced medication raise several ethical concerns. Swedlow (2003) raises the issue that restored competency through forced medication is "artificial." The view of these critics is that antipsychotic medications simply mask the more florid symptoms of psychosis, leaving the patient uncured and his or her incompetent status merely "muted" for the duration of treatment. Moreover, under such a view, antipsychotic medications interfere with the thinking and expression of an individual—potentially implicating First and Sixth Amendment concerns. Therefore, the competency that accompanies their administration is a false competency.

A second issue of concern is the use of antipsychotic drugs that have substantial and debilitating side effects. In *Washington v.*

Harper, the court recognized that the side effects to these drugs can be fatal and include a variety of motor control disorders, some treatable and some permanently disabling. While medical research in the 1990s resulted in a new class of antipsychotic medications that have fewer side effects, important ethical issues remain. First, it is unknown whether the administration of an antipsychotic drug, whether old or new, changes the way individuals actually think and express themselves. Second, the side effects may also change the individual's outward affect; a risk exists that this changed affect might prejudice the jury against the individual at trial. A heavily sedated defendant, for example, may give the appearance to the jury that he or she does not care about the outcome of the trial.

A third ethical issue concerns defendants who fail, after long periods of treatment, to regain competence. The *United States v. Sell* decision does not directly state whether the government must restore the defendant's competence in a reasonable period or cease its administration of the drug if the defendant is not dangerous. Yet defendants may continue to receive antipsychotic medications even when they are not dangerous and it is not possible to make them competent to stand trial. Cassel (2003) points to the case of Russell Weston, a schizophrenic man who stormed the U.S. Capitol in 1998 and killed two police officers. The Court of Appeals for the District of Columbia held that medication was appropriate because Weston was a danger to himself and others. Cassell notes that the ruling seems odd, for Weston, now chained to his bed in a solitary hospital room, is hardly a danger to self or others. Two years into forced medication, Weston still has not regained competence. Meanwhile, Cassell reports that Weston is suffering from some of the devastating effects of long-term psychotropic medication, including neurological dysfunction.

In sum, while the court articulated a set of standards for forced medication in competency to stand trial proceedings, the decision leaves unaddressed several issues that have served to continue the policy of criminalization of mentally ill defendants. Confined, restrained defendants may no longer be a danger to self or others yet may continue to be forcibly medicated.

COMPETENT TO BE EXECUTED

Thus far, this chapter has considered the conflict between criminal law and behavioral science concerning the defendant's competence from arrest to the end of trial proceedings. However, one of the most controversial recent issues concerns defendants who receive the death penalty but are incompetent at the time of their scheduled execution. Constitutionally, can we execute incompetent defendants? What standard should we use to assess competence to be executed? A second related question is whether the Constitution permits the forced administration of medication to make an inmate competent for execution. If the involuntary use of medication for competence for execution is legal, what are the ethical issues faced by psychiatrists and physicians asked to administer such medication?

The Constitution and Execution of the Seriously Mentally Ill

There are several reasons why an inmate may be incompetent at the time of execution. Certainly one reason is that a trial court incorrectly ruled the defendant competent to stand trial when, in fact, the defendant was seriously mentally ill and not competent. A jury may have convicted and sentenced such a defendant to death. A second reason concerns the deterioration in an inmate's mental condition while incarcerated. As discussed in chapter 1, prisons frequently do not provide adequate mental health treatment, and in the case of a prisoner sentenced to death, several years may lapse between the sentence and the exhaustion of an inmate's appeals. In this time, the inmate's mental condition may substantially deteriorate.

In *Ford v. Wainwright* (477 U.S. 399 [1986]), the U.S. Supreme Court ruled that the Eighth Amendment, which prohibits "cruel and unusual" punishment, does not permit the government to execute a prisoner who lacks a factual understanding of why the government wishes to execute him. This decision means that we may not execute a mentally incompetent inmate. Why does the Constitution prohibit such an execution? What, exactly, does this requirement mean? What does a prisoner need to understand about the impending execution? To answer these questions, we must look to the rationale presented in the *Ford v. Wainwright* decision regarding the purposes of punishment.

A psychiatrist who interviewed Ford, who was convicted of murder, testified at his trial about his mental illness. He stated that Ford had "no understanding of why he was being executed, made no connection between the homicide of which he had been convicted and the death penalty, and indeed seriously believed that he would not be executed because he owned the prisons and could control the Governor though his mind waves" (*Ford v. Wainwright,* 403). In deciding the case, the Supreme Court emphasized the lack of "retributive value [in] executing a person who has no comprehension of why he has been singled out and stripped of his fundamental right to life" (*Ford v. Wainwright,* 409). However, the court did not address what standard the Eighth Amendment requires. Does it require the kind of rational understanding enunciated in *Dusky,* or is a lower level of competency sufficient?

In 2007, the Supreme Court decided a case that presents precisely this question—the standard required for deciding when a person is competent to be executed. In *Panetti v. Dretke,* Scott Louis Panetti stood trial for murdering his wife's parents. Panetti had a decade-long history of hospitalizations for mental illness before the murders, but the trial court determined that he was competent to stand trial. The trial court permitted him to represent himself in his own capital murder case, in which he dressed like a cowboy and behaved in a bizarre fashion. The jury convicted him and sentenced him to death. His lawyers argued that his mental condition deteriorated while on death row. Shortly before his scheduled execution date, his lawyers petitioned the state court for a determination of his competency to be executed. Two mental health experts examined Panetti and concluded he was mentally competent to be executed, a finding accepted by the judge without holding a competency hearing. Panetti's lawyers then filed an appeal in federal court. After hearing testimony from four expert witnesses, a federal judge found that Panetti suffered some form of mental illness marked by delusions, including the delusion that his execution is being carried out through a conspiracy of demonic forces (*Panetti v. Dretke*, 401 F. Sup. 2d 702, 709 [W.D. Tex. 2004]). However, the judge nevertheless found that he had awareness of his pending execution and that he had committed the murders for which he received the death penalty. Therefore, the court ruled that he was mentally competent to be executed and a U.S. Appeals Court upheld the ruling (*Panetti v. Dretke*, 448 F. 3d 815 [5th Cir. 2006]).

In 2007, the Supreme Court ruled that the state could not execute Panetti since he lacked a rational understanding of why the government wished to execute him. Citing the *Ford* case, the court held that the Eight Amendment against cruel and unusual punishment bars execution of a defendant who is unaware of the reasons for his impending execution. Concluding that executing an insane defendant conflicts with common notions of decency and the established principle that condemned prisoners should be of sound mind to be able to prepare themselves for death, the court ruled that execution of an insane prisoner serves no retributive purpose. In his dissent, however, Justice Thomas argued that historically, competency to be executed never meant anything more than a rudimentary understanding by the condemned prisoner of why the death penalty was being imposed, citing the *Ford* court's declaration that as long as a prisoner understands why the state wishes to execute him, the retributive goal of punishment is met. In other words, the disagreement between the majority and dissenting opinions rested upon what the concept "awareness" meant and whether the Constitution requires a rational understanding in addition to a mere factual one (*Panetti v. Quarterman*, 127 S. Ct. 2842 [2007]).

Forced Medication and Competent to Be Executed

Where a state seeks to forcibly medicate an incompetent defendant sentenced to death, there cannot be a claim that the forced medication rests on medical necessity or even prison safety. In such cases, the state argues that its rights to carry out a criminal sentence outweigh any rights of the mentally ill

---

FOCUS 3.4. INCOMPETENCE AND THE
DEATH PENALTY

In 2006, the Texas Court of Appeals declined to hear the appeal of Steven Kenneth Staley. A federal district court ordered that Staley, a death-row inmate who is so severely mentally ill as to be unable to comprehend his situation, can be forcibly medicated so he can be executed while mentally competent. Staley is appealing the decision to the U.S. Supreme Court.

In 2006, a federal district court in Tennessee sided with the state and found that Gregory Thompson was competent to be executed. Thompson's lawyers appealed the decision to the Sixth Circuit federal appellate court, arguing that any semblance of competency achieved is by the use of powerful medication administered against his will.

For more information about these cases, consult the National Coalition to Abolish the Death Penalty Web site at http://www.ncadp.org/.

individual to refuse treatment. Several states have recently executed incompetent defendants, see, for example, Focus 3.4. The Supreme Court has never addressed the medication question in a capital case ruling. In 2003, in the case of convicted murderer Charles L. Singleton, the court let stand an Eighth Circuit appeals-court ruling that there is no constitutional barrier to force medication on an inmate for the purposes of execution. Singleton, who suffered from schizophrenia, was administered psychotropic drugs against his will because he was a danger to himself and others (*Singleton v. Norris,* 319 F 3d 1018 [8th Cir.]). The state of Arkansas executed Singleton in 2004.

Ethical Issues for Psychiatrists

Psychiatrist Howard Zonata (2003) notes that the *Ford v. Wainwright* case led the psychiatric profession to search for a set of guidelines for psychiatrists who might be called on to evaluate and/or treat psychotic death row inmates. The issue of concern was the ethical responsibilities for psychiatrists when treating inmates who no longer appreciate why the criminal justice system is punishing them or even that they will die because of their execution. The American Psychiatric Association (APA) and the American Medical Association (AMA) struggled to give guidance to physicians, and develop a set of guidelines, which remain controversial for some physicians. The AMA has defined participation in an execution as unethical, and in the early 1990s, they clarified the actions that constituted participation. The AMA Council on Ethical and Judicial Affairs stated that forcing medication on a condemned inmate solely to restore competence was unethical. However, physicians may treat inmates to mitigate suffering. The AMA leaves the ultimate decision to the treating physician (American Medical Association Council 1998). The decision turns on whether the physician is administering the medication to treat the patient's mental illness or whether the physician is acting as an agent of the state to further the execution.

CONCLUSION: THE THEORY AND
REALITY OF COMPETENCE

Courts order more competency evaluations for defendants and use more financial resources for their evaluation, adjudication, and treatment than for any other class of forensic activities (Golding 1992). Research also indicates that evaluations for competence to stand trial represent the most common type of referral for criminal forensic assessments (Cruise and Rogers 1998, 35). Roesch et al. (1999, 340) report that courts refer between 2 and 8 percent of all felony defendants for competency evaluations, and Bonnie and Grisso (2000) estimate that courts order approximately 60,000 competency evaluations annually in the United States. Defendants found incompetent to stand trial make up the largest group of psychiatric patients committed to mental hospitals by way of the criminal justice system (Pendleton 1980).

In theory, the requirement that a criminal defendant be mentally competent before the trial can proceed assures that the defendant will receive a fair trial. However, there are many sources of disagreement between criminal law and behavioral science concerning the standard for competency, and the ethical use of forced medication to restore competency for trial and for execution. And it can be argued that a determination of incompetent to stand trial is not a benefit to those accused: a ruling that the defendant is incompetent deprives the defendant of any trial until restored to competency. Critics of our treatment of mentally ill defendants note that for some defendants this means that they will forever remain in limbo as "accused" (Morris, Haroun, and Naimark 2004, 194–98). While a mentally incompetent defendant is presumed to be innocent of the crime until convicted, in reality, unlike other presumed innocent defendants who are released on bail until they stand trial, incompetent criminal defendants are routinely confined in maximum-security wards of state mental hospitals until they become competent.

CHAPTER 4

The Problems with the Insanity Defense

THE CONFLICT BETWEEN LAW AND PSYCHIATRY

I realized it was time to be punished . . . for
not being a good mother.

—Andrea Yates*

ON JUNE 20, 2001, at 9:48 A.M., Andrea Yates
called 911 and asked for assistance. She also called her husband
at work and told him that he needed to come home, but would
not say why. When her husband asked if anyone was hurt, Andrea
Yates responded that the kids were hurt. He asked, "Which
ones?" She responded, "All of them." Within minutes of her 911
call, several police officers arrived at the Yates home and discovered four dead children, soaking wet, covered with a sheet, lying
on Andrea Yates's bed. The fifth child was still in the bathtub,
floating face down.

A few hours later, Yates gave a seventeen-minute confession
to police sergeant Eric Mehl that detailed what had happened.

---

*Excerpts from Andrea Yates's full interview with Houston Police
Sergeant Eric Mehl at the Houston, Texas police station, conducted
on the afternoon of June 20, 2001 (*HoustonChronicle.com,* February
21, 2002, http://www.chron.com/disp/story.mpl/special/drownings/
1266294.html).

In the confession, she stated that she was not being a good mother to her children and that her children were not developing correctly in terms of their learning and their behavior. She indicated that it was time for her to receive punishment, and she wanted the criminal justice system to punish her for not being a good mother.

Two indictments charged Andrea Yates with capital murder for the drowning deaths of three of her five children. She entered a plea of not guilty because she was insane at the time of the killings. Texas law defines insanity as an affirmative defense that, "at the time of the conduct charged, the actor, as a result of severe mental disease or defect, did not know that his conduct was wrong" (Insanity, Texas Penal Code, §8.01, 2006).

At trial, ten psychiatrists and two psychologists gave testimony about Yates's mental state at the time of the killings as well as her history of mental illness. Her medical history included hospitalizations for attempted suicide, depression, and delusions; the most recent hospitalization had occurred on March 31, 2001. Four of the psychiatrists and one of the psychologists had treated her either in a medical facility or as a private patient before June 20, 2001. They testified regarding the symptoms, severity, and treatment of Andrea Yates's mental illness. Five psychiatrists and one psychologist saw Yates on or soon after June 20 for assessment and/or treatment of her mental illness. Four of these five psychiatrists and the psychologist testified that on June 20, 2001, she did not know right from wrong, was incapable of knowing that what she did was wrong, or believed that her acts were right. The fifth psychiatrist testified that she had not made a determination regarding Andrea Yates's ability to know whether her actions were wrong; however, she testified that given Andrea Yates's belief that the children would perish in the fires of hell, she believed that their drowning was the right thing to do.

The tenth psychiatrist was the state's sole mental health expert in the case. He testified that although Andrea Yates was psychotic on June 20, she knew that what she did was wrong. He reasoned that because she said that her thoughts were coming from Satan, she must have known that they were wrong. He testified that if she believed she was saving her children, she would have shared her plan with others rather than hide it as she did, and that if she really believed that Satan was going to harm the children, she would have called the police or a pastor or would have sent the children away. He also indicated that she covered the bodies out of guilt or shame (*Yates v. State,* 171 S.W. 3d 215 [2005]).

The jury found Yates guilty and assessed punishment of life in prison. However, following the verdict and before the punishment phase of the trial, defense counsel learned that the state's mental health expert had presented false testimony in the case. More specifically, the state's expert testified that he was a consultant with a television show that Yates was known to watch. At trial, the expert testified that an episode that aired shortly before June 21, 2001, depicted a woman with postpartum depression who drowned her children in a bathtub and the jury in that case found the woman insane. Defense counsel learned that no episode with such a plot had aired on the television show and moved for a mistrial. The trial court rejected the motion. On appeal, in *Yates v. Texas* (171 S.W. 3d 215 [Tex. Crim. App. 2005]), the Court of Appeals of Texas reversed and remanded the case, finding that there was a reasonable likelihood that the expert's false testimony could have affected the judgment of the jury and that the false testimony affected the substantial rights of Yates.

In June 2006, once again, Andrea Yates faced trial, and she asserted the defense of not guilty by reason of insanity. Using the same Texas standard for insanity, the jury unanimously found Yates not guilty because of insanity. On July 27, 2006, a *New York Times* article reported that when asked by the press to explain the verdict, the jury foreman stated, "We understand that she knew it was legally wrong," he said. "But in her delusional mind,

FOCUS 4.1. ANDREA YATES'S 911 CALL

Shortly after Andrea Yates drowned her five children on June 20, 2001, she dialed 911 and had the following conversation with the dispatcher.

911: What's your name?

YATES: Andrea Yates.

911: What's the problem?

YATES: Um, I just need them to come.

911: Is your husband there?

YATES: No.

911: Well, what's the problem?

YATES: I need them to come.

911: I need to know why we're coming, ma'am. Is he standing there next to you?

YATES: Pardon me.

911: Are you having a disturbance? Are you ill? Or what?

YATES: Yes, I'm ill.

911: Do you need an ambulance?

YATES: No, I need a police officer. Yeah, send an ambulance.

911: What's the problem?

YATES: Um. . . .

911: Is someone burglarizing your house? I mean, what is it?

YATES: [Heavy breathing]

911: What kind of medical problem do you have?

911: Hello.

YATES: I just need a police officer.

911: Are you at [address], right?

YATES: Yes.

911: Are you there alone?

YATES: Yes.

911: Andrea Yates?

YATES: Yes.

911: Is your husband there with you?

YATES: No.

911: Okay, well, why do you need the police, ma'am?

YATES: I just need them to be here.

911: For what?

YATES: I just need them to come.

911: You sure you're alone?

YATES: No, my sister's here.

When police arrived at the Yates home, they found no other adults with Andrea.

———

Adapted from "911 Tape Reveals Unemotional Andrea Yates," CNN.com, January 6, 2002, at http://archives.cnn.com/2001/US/12/10/yates.911/index.html.

---

in her severely mentally ill mind, we believe that she thought what she did was right."

CRIMINAL RESPONSIBILITY AND THE CLAIM OF INSANITY

The insanity defense concerns the extent to which a person accused of a crime may be relieved of criminal responsibility by virtue of mental disease. It rests on a socially constructed belief that we should punish persons for criminal acts only when they are blameworthy for those acts. However, as the Andrea Yates case illustrates, how society decides to define blameworthiness is a controversial issue. In Yates's first trial, the jury decided that regardless of her history of mental illness, she was blameworthy for the deaths of her children. The jury decided to take into account her mental illness when they gave her a sentence of life without parole instead of sentencing her to death. By the time of her retrial, however, the media had focused a great deal of attention on Yates's history of mental illness. Many legal scholars and mental health experts had spoken to the media about the injustice of holding Yates criminally responsible. The media also presented a great deal of information about postpartum psychosis and depression. In the second trial, the jury appeared to discard the definition of insanity in Texas law and instead focused on a more complex understanding of mental illness than simply whether Yates knew that her actions were legally wrong. The difference between the first and second verdicts illustrates the confusion about what should count as insanity and how different claims about what counts can lead to contradictory verdicts.

In this chapter, we will first examine the historical development of the insanity defense and the controversies between law and medicine regarding its conceptualization. Notice, for example, that Texas law only permitted an acquittal of not guilty by reason of insanity "if the actor, as a result of severe mental disease or defect, did not know that his conduct was wrong" (Insanity, Texas Penal Code, §8.01, 2006). This definition is a narrow legal standard that restricts how juries can evaluate a defendant's behavior at the time of the crime. It represents an attempt by a legislature to use moral language as the definition of insanity rather than psychiatric categories. As we will discuss, defining insanity in terms of moral values has a long historical tradition; however, the Texas definition presents an atypical moral definition in contrast to definitions used during earlier historical periods. This narrowing of the criteria for insanity developed, in part, because of negative public sentiment about defendants who successfully asserted the insanity defense. Public opinion shifted to the idea that too many individuals were escaping punishment because they were "faking insanity," even though empirical evidence indicated otherwise (Perlin 2000,

231–37). In particular, public sentiment was especially negative after John Hinckley successfully used the defense at his trial for the attempted assassination of President Ronald Reagan.

Second, this chapter will consider the kind of evidence offered in the *Yates* case and insanity cases in general. In the *Yates* case, experts for both the defense and prosecution agreed that Yates was seriously mentally ill at the time she killed her children. Indeed, the defense presented a great deal of evidence concerning her history of mental illness that included a long history of treatment by psychiatrists and psychologists. However, the language of psychiatry is different from the language of law. Psychiatry speaks of disorders and syndromes while law speaks of criminal responsibility and insanity. How do lawyers, experts, judges, and juries move from one domain to another in a court of law? What controversies arise because of the different languages of law and psychiatry? How should juries evaluate the opinion of experts concerning the defendant's mental state at the time of the crime?

Finally, this chapter will examine the difficulties in reforming American laws concerning insanity because of the priority given to the societal values of free will, individual accountability, and punishment. Critics maintain that the priority of those values creates doctrinal confusion about what counts as insanity because of the various insanity standards used in different states and the subordination of modern psychiatry and psychology to outdated conceptions of the mind. We will also examine the arguments of scholars who favor retaining the emphasis on free will and individual accountability. These scholars contend that science is not superior to morality and that moral values should prevail in deciding what counts as insanity.

The Development of the Insanity Defense Doctrine

Insanity is a social and legal term rather than a medical/psychiatric one. However, in our contemporary society, a person who claims the defense of insanity relies on psychiatric terms and experts to attempt to prove that defense, and the prosecution uses its own experts to counter the defendant's insanity defense. Therefore, two different models or claims about the nature of the individual and society are present in insanity pleas. There is the model of criminal law, grounded in the assumption of free will and the responsibility of individuals for their actions, and there is the model of the behavioral sciences, especially psychiatry and psychology, grounded in the assumption of determinism and a cause-and-effect view of the reasons for behavior. These two claims about human behavior create conflict between law and psychiatry regarding how criminal law should define insanity and the role of the behavioral sciences in that formulation. Perhaps we should formulate insanity standards and definitions on the basis of scientific research gained from the behavioral sciences concerning mental illness. Alternatively, perhaps we should base insanity standards exclusively on moral standards of ordinary persons who believe in free will and use their intuitive sense of justice to decide whether to hold a person blameworthy. In order to understand this controversy, we will review the development of the insanity defense doctrine in our society and then consider the controversies concerning how we define insanity today.

Early Doctrine

Scholars trace the origins of our American conception of the insanity plea to the legal system of pre-Norman England in which the system of justice initially relied on a secular code based on principles of compensation and retaliation (N. Walker 1968; Finkel 1988). If a person committed a wrong, the legal system held that person responsible and expected the person to compensate the victim. This was a system based on strict liability, in which only the outer conduct of the accused was relevant; the legal system did not consider thoughts and motivations necessary for conviction. It was, therefore, irrelevant whether a person intended the action; the law only considered the harm to the victim. The status of the victim and the seriousness of the harm determined the compensation paid to the victim rather than the extent to which the offender was to blame. However, ecclesiastical law, a system that developed alongside the secular system, developed a concern with establishing responsibility for sin. It linked blameworthiness to "inner facts" that, in the Church's view, courts should consider and weigh before moral guilt was established. These "inner facts" would demonstrate the person's wickedness or immorality. This was an early formulation of our conception of *mens rea*—the idea that it was unjust to stigmatize a person as a criminal unless an evil or guilty mind accompanied that person's evil deed.

From the moment a person's "inner facts" became important, the mental state of a person became important to consider; that is, it became necessary to account for those who could not think like other individuals and who the law should not blame. These were the insane. Under ecclesiastical law, the judiciary did not hold the insane as criminally responsible and did not punish them because the judges held that the insane could not tell the difference between good and evil. Insanity represented a defect of the mind that prevented the accused from exercising free will when they committed criminal acts. The law thus separated the sick from the bad based upon a person's capacity to discern good from evil. Gradually, England developed a separate system of criminal law that contained criminal defenses. In the case of defendants who claimed insanity, rather than simply looking at whether the accused could form *mens rea,* the law required the accused to assert insanity as a defense to the criminal act (N. Walker 1968, 15–34; Finkel 1988, 3–7; Goldstein 1967, 9–11).

English common law continued to emphasize the idea that the criminal law should not hold the insane responsible for their crimes because they lacked free will and did not have guilty or evil minds. Sir Matthew Hale, lord chief justice of England, devoted an entire chapter in the *History of the Pleas of the Crown* (1736/2003) to examining madness and lunacy in reference to criminal offenses and punishments. Hale was not only a lawyer but well informed about psychological theories. Hale distinguished "lunacy" with "lucid" intervals from "permanent madness." Both lunacy and permanent madness qualified for the plea of insanity. However, Hale argued that there are also situations in which there is a partial insanity of mind. He believed that if the partially insane individual had enough understanding, equivalent to the child at the discretionary age of twelve or fourteen, then the person was guilty (Walker 1968, 35–41).

Two notable cases in England illustrate the controversial nature of the insanity defense in terms of what mental states should count as insanity and whether moral or medical ideas should prevail in insanity claims. In *Rex v. Arnold* (16 How. St. Tr. 695 [1724]), the jury found Ned Arnold guilty of shooting and wounding Lord Onslow even though the defense presented a great deal of testimony concerning Arnold's alleged madness. The case is significant for Justice Tracy's instructions to the jury in which he described the need for caution in excusing someone from punishment because of a claim of insanity. He advised that exemption from punishment required "a total deprivation of understanding and memory" that demonstrated that the accused did not know what he was doing "no more than an infant, than a brute or a wild beast" (N. Walker 1968, 56). Justice Tracy's admonition to the jury was widely quoted as the "wild beast" test for insanity. It signals a skeptical attitude about claims for insanity and a formulation that attempts to limit the kind of mental states that count as insanity in court. In the second case, *Rex v. Hadfield* (27 How. St. Tr. 1286 [1800]), defense counsel successfully challenged the idea of a "total deprivation of memory and understanding" as the standard for insanity. James Hadfield faced trial for the attempted shooting of King George III. While Hadfield knew what he was doing and knew that murder was wrong, his insanity defense rested on his delusion that his mission was to rid the world of King George III before the Second Coming of Christ. In arguing against the "wild beast test," Hadfield's defense counsel, supported by testimony from physicians, contended that insanity should include those persons deluded by false premises. These individuals had a diseased brain that could have lucid and delusive moments over which they had no control (N. Walker 1968, 75–83).

These two cases illustrate the dilemmas that remain with us today. Justice Tracy's caution about excusing someone from punishment unless the person displays a total deprivation of mind expresses the claim of criminal law that if a person can still exercise what the law considers as free will, the law should hold that person criminally responsible. Central to this claim is a skeptical attitude about insanity claims, the role of punishment in maintaining the social order, and the disruption to the social order that would occur if society failed to punish persons who claim insanity but appear to have some use of cognition and reasoning ability. Hadfield's case introduces a more complex view as to what counts as insanity than the one presented by the "wild beast test." In this more complex view, the claim of insanity does not derive simply from whether the accused knew what they were doing or whether it was wrong. Presenting the issue as a "diseased brain" begins to articulate a different kind of claim about insanity, one that advances the idea that what should count as insanity are mental illnesses that the medical profession should define and diagnose, and that they should warrant consideration at trial.

The M'Naghten Rules

One of the most controversial and important insanity cases in English and American law is the trial of Daniel M'Naghten (10 Clark and Finnelly 200 [1843]), who was accused of murdering Edward Drummond. M'Naghten's insanity claim concerned his belief that he was being persecuted by a political party, the

Tories, for voting against them in an election. He decided to kill
the prime minister, but he mistakenly shot Edward Drummond,
believing him to be the prime minister. At trial, nine medical
witnesses testified that M'Naghten was a paranoiac entangled
in an elaborate system of delusions and that he held the prime
minister responsible for his continual financial and personal
misfortunes. Defense counsel argued that M'Naghten's insanity
was much like Hadfield's; that is, M'Naghten had reasoned with
faulty premises. During the trial, they quoted from several medical sources, including the work of an American doctor, Isaac
Ray, who published one of the most influential books on the
subject of insanity, *A Treatise on the Medical Jurisprudence of Insanity* (1838/1983). Ray was an outspoken general practitioner who
attacked tests such as "ability to tell right from wrong," or "delusional thinking" as too narrow to assess criminal responsibility.
Instead, he proposed that we exempt the accused from punishment if "the mental unsoundness . . . embraced the criminal act"
(N. Walker 1968, 90). Ray clearly envisioned a greater role for
science, and particularly medicine, in criminal law.

The jury was persuaded by the evidence presented by the
defense and found M'Naghten not guilty by reason of insanity.
M'Naghten spent the remainder of his life at the Broadmoor
mental institution. However, Queen Victoria, the House of Lords,
and the public disapproved of the verdict because it permitted
M'Naghten to escape punishment when he knew at the time
of the crime that what he was doing was wrong. The House of
Lords asked the judges of the common law courts to respond to
a series of questions on insanity. The judges' responses, known as
the M'Naghten rules, included a rule that defined insanity. This
definition ignored the recent understanding in mental disorders
reflected in the *Hadfield* and *M'Naghten* decisions and the views
of medical authorities such as Ray. Instead, the M'Naghten rule
asked whether the accused "was labouring under such defect of
reason, from disease of the mind as not to know the nature and

quality of the act he was doing; or, if he did know it, that he did not know he was doing what was wrong" (*M'Naghten's Case,* 10 Clark and Finnelly 210).

This case illustrates how public sentiment can lead to changes in legal rules even though these rules may not reflect current scientific knowledge about the phenomenon of concern. In particular, the insanity standard enunciated by the M'Naghten rules ignored affective and impulsive behavior that medical authorities at that time considered important in an insanity standard. Instead, it provided a defense only for individuals with a cognitive impairment; that is, an accused can seek an insanity acquittal if a disease of the mind affected his ability to know right from wrong or the nature and quality of the act he was doing. This represents a retrenchment to the absence of free will construction of insanity. The medical community at the time was concerned that the M'Naghten rules were formulated around a theory of mind that had been discredited by research, one that viewed the mind as divided into separate compartments that could function independently of the other (Boland 1999, 15–17). Additionally, the rules leave critical words and phases undefined. The phrases "disease of mind" and "nature of the act" are undefined, as is the word "know." However, in spite of these criticisms and concerns, by 1851 the federal courts and most of the state courts in the United States adopted the M'Naghten rules for defining insanity (Simon and Aaronson 1988, 14).

The Irresistible Impulse Rule

The debate over whether "irresistible impulse" should constitute a legitimate insanity claim is another example of the conflict between law and medicine. This conflict emerged in the latter part of the nineteenth century when medical professionals sought to include additional diseases under an insanity test in accordance with current medical research (Boland 1999, 49–50; Finkel 1988, 30–33). Accepted medical facts, the medical community argued, described a mental illness (impulsive insanity) whose symptoms were emotional and volitional incapacity. The claim was that this disease of the mind often left reason (cognition) undisturbed; however, individuals had an inability to control their behavior. Medicine used terms such as "moral insanity" and "instinctive madness" to describe this disease of the mind in which an impulse is accompanied by consciousness but is, in some instances, irresistible.

Advocates for an irresistible impulse rule argued that that the criminal law should not hold individuals with such a mental illness responsible for their criminal acts. Their arguments were persuasive. In *Smith v. Commonwealth* (1 Duvall 226 [Ky. 1864]), the Kentucky Court of Appeals found that a person could be legally insane if he knew wrong from right but had a paralyzed "moral will" that "impelled" him to do what was "forbidden." In an Alabama case, *Parsons v. Alabama* (2 So. 854 [1887]), the court stated that the law of criminal responsibility had not kept pace with the advances of medical science. It held that criminal responsibility contained two elements: "capacity of intellectual discrimination" and "freedom of will," and that a just and reasonable test of responsibility must take into account both elements, clearly indicating that the court considered "irresistible impulse" a valid marker of insanity. The court also noted that it was a question of fact, not of law, whether insanity can so affect the mind "as to subvert the freedom of the will, and thereby destroy the power of the victim to choose between the right and wrong, although he perceives it" (81 Ala. 588). In *Davis v. United States* (165 U.S. 373 [1897]), the Supreme Court upheld the trial court's jury instruction that an accused was insane if "though conscious of (the nature of the act) and able to distinguish between right and wrong ... yet his will, by which I mean the governing power of his mind, has been otherwise than voluntarily so completely destroyed that his actions are not subject to it, but are beyond his control" (165 U.S. 378).

Eighteen states and the federal system added an irresistible impulse rule to the M'Naghten rule, signaling the greater influence of science, particularly psychiatry, in criminal trials. However, lawyers, judges, and legal scholars quickly became skeptical of the irresistible impulse rule, charging that it was too much of an expansion of the M'Naghten rules, impossible to apply, and without scientific basis (Goldstein 1967, 68). In 1982, the American Psychiatric Association's *Statement on the Insanity Defense* concluded, "The line between an irresistible impulse and an impulse not resisted is probably no sharper than that between twilight and dusk" (American Psychiatric Association 1982, 11). Critics argued that it was impossible to diagnose reliably whether an impulse was irresistible in a particular defendant.

The Durham Rule

The Durham rule, also known as the "product test," reflected an increasing authority of the medical profession over criminal trials because this rule permits a medical definition of insanity. The rule provides that the law should excuse an accused from criminal responsibility if the person's act was the product of mental disease or defect. New Hampshire first enunciated a product test in 1845, reflecting the influence of Isaac Ray on New Hampshire judicial thinking. However, the product test gained prominence in the United States in the 1954 case of *Durham v. United States* (214 F.2d 862 [1954]). In *Durham,* Judge Bazelon held "that an accused is not criminally responsible if his unlawful act was the product of mental disease or mental defect" (214 F.2d 874–75). In doing so, Judge Bazelon overruled the M'Naghten rules supplemented by the irresistible impulse rule that had prevailed until then in the District of Columbia. Rather, under the Durham rule the focus is whether the mental disorder caused the offender's actions; that is, if the crime was an offspring of the psychiatric impairment, then the defendant was not guilty by reason of insanity.

The Durham rule reflected optimism about the arrival of a new reformative era of treatment of the mentally ill instead of the previous concern with deterrence and retribution (Boland 1999, 63–64). The intent was to move the mentally ill from the criminal justice system to the mental health system. The Durham rule also signaled an increased role for psychiatry in criminal trials. Under the Durham rule, ideally, medical experts would provide expert testimony on mental disease or defect and the jury would determine the ultimate question of whether the act was the product. In addition, unlike the irresistible impulse rule, the Durham rule did not attempt to crystallize one set of medical theories in place of another but rather was a broad rule, designed to embrace future developments in psychiatry. The courts were convinced that this new rule would usher in a new era of harmony between psychiatrists and lawyers.

The optimism, however, was short-lived. The application of the new test in the District of Columbia led to much criticism over how to determine what acts were products of a mental disorder and even how to define whether a disease or a defect actually existed (Goldstein 1967, 83–92). Other courts feared that the concept of mental illness was so broad that it might encompass all serious criminals, especially psychopaths—persons with personality disorders marked by antisocial thought and behavior. While psychiatrists might consider psychopaths as falling within the classifications of mental disorders, courts viewed psychopaths as evil, dangerous, and hardened criminals who were fully aware of their actions. They refused to adopt the Durham rule, indicating a skeptical attitude about psychiatry's status as a science and rejecting a deterministic view of human behavior.

There were several other areas of concern with the Durham rule (Boland 1999, 66–68). First, judges and lawyers believed the test gave too much power to the psychiatric world because psychiatrists were now able to testify very broadly about mental illnesses and their effects rather than being restricted to the issue of whether the defendant's mental illness weakened his knowledge of right and wrong. Second, in the four years after *Durham,* the number of acquittals from insanity pleas in the District of Columbia rose to 150, and the public perceived that the Durham rule was responsible. A final concern was the condition of mental hospitals where indeterminate confinement took place. Critics charged that these hospitals were really prisons in disguise with only a pretense of treatment and a gross disregard for civil liberties and due process. Lawsuits ensued that led to the release of some of those acquitted on the grounds of insanity to the community in relatively short times. Their release fostered grave, if incorrect, public concerns for safety. Even Judge Bazelon announced that he was abandoning the Durham rule in the case of *United States v. Brawner* (471 F.2d 969 [1972]). He proposed a new test for the District of Columbia that tied the defendant's responsibility to the degree of impairment of his mental or emotional processes or behavior controls at the time of the crime.

The ALI Rule

The American Law Institute (ALI), an organization of judges, lawyers, and legal scholars formed in 1923 to improve the law and its administration, began a study in the 1950s to consider how to phrase a comprehensive insanity test. In 1962, ALI drafted a model penal code test for criminal responsibility. ALI rejected the advice of its own psychiatric committee that favored the Durham rule. Instead, it proposed a test that included elements of the M'Naghten and irresistible impulse rules but with new words for both parts:

(1) A person is not responsible for criminal conduct if at the time of such conduct as a result of mental disease or defect he lacks substantial capacity either to appreciate the criminality [wrongfulness] of his conduct or to conform his conduct to the requirements of law.

(2) As used in this article, the terms "mental disease or defect" do not include an abnormality manifested only be repeated criminal or otherwise antisocial conduct. (American Law Institute 1962)

The ALI rule was significant because it excused cognitively *or* volitionally impaired offenders; therefore, the rule did not require both symptoms. In addition, the drafters of the ALI rule tried to correct the earlier language problems of previous rules. Notice that the ALI rule substituted the term "appreciate" for the M'Naghten term "to know" and the phrase "criminality of his conduct" clearly indicates that insanity concerns a "legal wrong" rather than a moral one. In addition, the phrase "he lacks substantial capacity" clarified that the ALI test eliminated the requirement of total insanity. Finally, when it came to the "irresistible impulse" part of the test, ALI substituted "to conform his conduct to the requirements of the law." However, the terms "mental disease or defect" remain undefined and "capacity to conform" raised some of the same concerns as the irresistible impulse rule.

Federal courts and many state courts adopted the ALI rule. In 1961, only one state had a standard similar to the ALI rule. By 1985, approximately half of the states used the ALI rule either verbatim or with slight modifications. The success of the ALI rule signaled a counterreaction by the legal profession to the attempt by psychiatrists to gain more control over criminal trials (Goldstein 1967, 92). The return to the basic ideas contained in the M'Naghten and irresistible impulse rules gave the legal profession, once again, a set of familiar assumptions about human behavior tied to *mens rea, actus reus,* and free will.

The Insanity Defense Reform Act of 1984

On March 30, 1981, there was an assassination attempt on President Ronald Reagan. At trial, his assailant, John Hinckley pled insanity as his defense. His claim of insanity centered on his infatuation with a movie star, Jodie Foster. Approximately four years prior to the attempted assassination, Hinckley saw the move *Taxi Driver* several times and became obsessed with Foster, who played a prostitute in the movie. Hinckley never developed any meaningful contact with Foster; rather, he decided that he could gain her respect and love if he achieved notoriety by assassinating the president. He initially started to follow President Gerald Ford; however, President Reagan became his eventual target.

At the time that Hinckley shot Reagan, the insanity standard in the District of Columbia was the ALI rule. The word "appreciate" in the rule's assessment of whether the accused "lacks substantial capacity ... to appreciate the criminality of his conduct" became a critical issue in the trial of Hinckley. The defense argued successfully that "appreciate" not only meant cognitive awareness but included an emotional understanding of the consequences of his actions. The defense maintained that Hinckley did not have an emotional understanding of the consequences of his actions at the time of the shooting. The defense called medical experts to testify about Hinckley's mental condition and presented writings that Hinckley had generated in the months preceding the shootings including a letter to Jodie Foster in order to portray a man who they claimed was totally without the mental capacity to appreciate the wrongfulness of his conduct or to conform his conduct to the requirements of the law. The prosecution also called medical experts as witnesses who testified that Hinckley knew what he was doing at the time of the shootings and was therefore legally sane. However, on June 21, 1981, the jury found Hinckley not guilty by reason of insanity (Bonnie, Jeffries, and Low 2000).

Hinckley's acquittal sparked public outrage about the insanity defense and created pressure for reform. Again, notice that the outrage concerns finding a defendant not guilty by reason of insanity when evidence indicates that the person knew what he or she was doing at the time of the crime; that is, Hinckley knew he was attempting to kill the president. In addition, criticism arose about the role of psychiatric/psychological testimony in insanity defense cases. As we will discuss later in this chapter, the legal community criticized the kind of testimony that mental health experts should provide in insanity defense cases.

Following the *Hinckley* verdict, various professional associations convened special committees to make recommendations about the insanity defense. The National Mental Health Association (Kelitz and Fulton 1984), the American Psychiatric Association (1983), and the American Bar Association (1983) recommended retaining the insanity defense. The American Medical Association (1984) favored abolishing the insanity defense and, instead, providing for acquittal when the defendant, because of mental disease or defect, lacks the state of mind (*mens rea*) required as an element of the offense charged.

Many changes to insanity pleas occurred because of criticism of the *Hinckley* verdict. At the federal level, Congress passed the Insanity Defense Reform Act (IDRA) of 1984. The IDRA supplanted the ALI rule and any other insanity standards used by other federal courts. The IDRA rule states:

> Affirmative defense. It is an affirmative defense to a prosecution under any Federal statute that, at the time of the commission of the acts constituting the offense, the defendant as a result of serious mental disease or defect, was unable to appreciate the nature and quality or wrongfulness of his acts. Mental disease or defect does not otherwise constitute a defense.
>
> Burden of proof. The defendant has the burden of proving the defense of insanity by clear and convincing evidence. (Insanity Defense, 18 U.S.C. §17 [2006])

Notice that the IDRA rule's provisions included changing "lacks substantial capacity to appreciate" to "unable to appreciate," indicating that to be declared insane requires total mental impairment. The IDRA rule also eliminated of any type of volitional (irresistible impulse) excuse to the criminal defense. In addition, this rule requires defendants to plead insanity as an affirmative defense. This means that the IDRA shifted the burden of proof: instead of the prosecution having to prove that the defendant was sane at the time of the act, the defense must prove that the defendant was insane. Moreover, the standard of proof that the defense must meet is the standard of "clear and convincing evidence." Clear and convincing evidence is a standard of proof in between "preponderance of the evidence" (more likely than not) and "beyond reasonable doubt" (a reasonable certainty). While the prosecution must prove the defendant's guilt using the standard of beyond reasonable doubt, the IDRA requires that the defense must prove not guilty by reason of insanity by clear and convincing evidence.

Post-Hinckley Reform of State Statutes

At the state level, largely because of the *Hinckley* case, thirty-four states changed their insanity defenses between 1982 and 1985 (Steadman, McGreevy et al. 1993, 32–44). However, there exists great variation in how states define insanity, and in some states, the defense was completely abolished. Alaska adopted solely a M'Naghten cognitive incapacity test while ten states (Arizona, Delaware, Indiana, Illinois, Louisiana, Maine, Ohio, South Carolina, South Dakota, and Texas) adopted solely a moral incapacity test. Fourteen states (Arkansas, Connecticut, District of Columbia, Georgia, Hawaii, Kentucky, Maryland, Massachusetts, Oregon, Rhode Island, Vermont, West Virginia, Wisconsin, and Wyoming) adopted some combination of the volitional incapacity and moral incapacity test. Three states (Michigan, New Mexico, and Virginia) combine a full M'Naghten test

FOCUS 4.2. THE SUPREME COURT AND THE
INSANITY DEFENSE

The United States Supreme Court rarely hears cases involving the insanity defense, but decided to hear the case of *Clark v. Arizona* (548 U.S. 735 [2006]).

During the early hours of June 21, 2000, seventeen-year-old Eric Clark, armed with a handgun, circled his pickup truck around a local neighborhood while playing loud music. After neighbors called the police, Flagstaff police officer Jeffrey Moritz responded to the scene. As Moritz approached the car, Clark fired several shots at Moritz and fled the scene. Shortly thereafter, police arrested Clark and charged him with first-degree murder for "intentionally or knowingly" causing the death of a police officer.

At trial, Clark did not deny that he shot and killed the police officer; rather, he asserted the affirmative defense of "guilty except insane" (Insanity Test, Ariz. Rev. Stat. § 13–502[A] 2006), which provides that the defendant must be "afflicted with a mental disease or defect of such severity that the person did not know the criminal act was wrong." Clark also argued that his mental illness prevented him from forming the criminal intent (mens rea) that the government was required to prove beyond a reasonable doubt.

The prosecution presented evidence that Clark had purposefully circled the neighborhood with the intention of confronting and killing a police officer. Clark introduced expert evidence that he was a diagnosed paranoid schizophrenic who believed that aliens had taken over his town. Experts testified that while he understood right from wrong, he was making that judgment in the context of an abnormal state of reality: he thought aliens were torturing him. At trial, the judge ruled that Arizona law confined the use of the expert evidence to his insanity claim and did not permit him to use it to show he could not form criminal intent. The court also ruled that he had not sufficiently proved his insanity, and convicted Clark and sentenced him to twenty-five years to life in prison. The Arizona Court of Appeals affirmed.

The Supreme Court considered two questions: first, whether Arizona's insanity law violated Clark's right to due process under the Fourteenth Amendment because Arizona did not define its insanity defense in terms of the M'Naghten rules, and second, whether Arizona's refusal to consider mental disease or defect to refute the element of criminal intent (mens rea) violated Clark's right to due process under the Fourteenth Amendment.

The court held that due process does not prohibit Arizona's use of an insanity test stated solely in terms of capacity to tell whether an act charged as a crime was right or wrong. The court stated that the M'Naghten rules are not a minimum standard that a government must provide, that no particular formulation of the insanity defense has evolved into a baseline rule for due process, and that the insanity rule, like the conceptualization of criminal offenses, is open to state choice. The court also ruled that Arizona could constitutionally limit the use of expert evidence about a defendant's mental disease and capacity to his insanity defense, noting that it serves to avoid juror confusion and juror misunderstanding.

with a volitional incapacity test. Only New Hampshire still uses the product test.

In addition, some states (Alaska, Delaware, Georgia, Illinois, Indiana, Kentucky, Michigan, New Mexico, Pennsylvania, South Carolina, and South Dakota) supplement the traditional "not guilty by reason of insanity" verdict with an alternative of "guilty but mentally ill." Usually a defendant found "guilty but mentally ill" will receive mental health treatment until assessed as mentally healthy, at which point he must serve the remainder of his imposed sentence. Finally, four states (Idaho, Kansas, Montana, and Utah) have no specific insanity defense possible. These states allow consideration of evidence of mental illness directly on the element of *mens rea* defining the offense (*Clark v. Arizona,* 548 U.S. 735 [2006]).

The variation in the legal terminology used to define insanity and its absence as a specific defense indicates doctrinal confusion concerning how the criminal justice system views persons who are mentally ill at the time they committed a crime. The definition of a law depends on the purpose(s) of the definer. Initially, the law defined a person judged as insane at the time of the crime as not blameworthy because an insane person was not considered to have the capacity to act as a free and responsible citizen. Therefore, the person was acquitted of the crime although acquittal usually meant that the court would order the defendant's commitment to a mental hospital. The post-Hinckley changes to insanity statutes demonstrate a high degree of public skepticism about insanity claims. One telephone survey shortly after the Hinckley trial's conclusion indicated that the public perceived the verdict as unfair. Respondents thought Hinckley sane at the time of the crime, they did not trust the psychiatrists' testimony at the trial, and the vast majority thought the insanity defense was a loophole. These attitudes may have been affected by a lack of understanding of the insanity defense: the respondents were unable to define the legal test for insanity and thought that the criminal justice system would confine Hinckley only a short time, contrary to the estimates of experts (Hans and Slater 1983). However, as the second Andrea Yates case demonstrates, juries are willing to find defendants not guilty by reason of insanity even when the defendant's behavior does not appear to fall within the language of the particular insanity statute, and when the accused appeared to act with some intentionality or planning in the commission of the crimes. These considerations raise the following questions: What kind of evidence should courts permit in cases where a defendant makes a claim of insanity? What is at issue when we find a person insane? The remainder of this chapter will consider these questions.

THE ROLE OF THE EXPERT WITNESS

The history of the various insanity tests illustrates the ambivalence that the law has concerning the role of behavioral science experts in criminal cases. The reluctance to define insanity in medical/psychiatric terminology matches the limited role given to mental health professionals in terms of their testimony in insanity defense cases. In insanity defense trials, typically both the prosecution and defense will call expert witnesses from the mental health community to testify regarding the mental state/illness of the defendant. From a scientific perspective, expert opinion is not mere conjecture or speculation; it is the expert's judgment on a matter of fact. It differs from lay witness testimony in that the expert has specialized training. However, despite the specialized training of psychiatrists and psychologists, there is continuing legal debate about the scientific validity of behavioral science, especially as applied to knowing the state of mind of the defendant at the time of the crime. Legal decision makers often express concern that the incorporation of psychiatric concepts into the criminal law impairs the law's ability to achieve its policy objectives. They fear that the mental health community will have undue influence on ultimate legal determinations and that the law will become dependent on concepts that belong to an outside discipline. In contrast, psychiatrists and psychologists express concern that courts will limit the testimony of psychiatrists and psychologists and will use outdated and erroneous conceptualizations of the mind and mental disease when making determinations regarding the defendant's insanity at the time of the criminal act. Historically, the debate concerning the role of the expert witness in insanity defense cases principally concerns whether the court should permit the medical expert to testify about the "ultimate issue" of whether the defendant was insane at the time of the criminal act.

The M'Naghten Rules and the Ultimate Issue

Simon and Aaronson (1988, 81–88) trace the origin of the ultimate issue question to the M'Naghten rules adopted in 1843. Under those rules, the focus is on the cognitive capacity of the defendant; the rule assumes a psychological theory of a mind divided into separate independent compartments, one of which could be diseased without affecting the others. The expert witness psychiatrist in a case relying on the application of the M'Naghten rules faces a dilemma regarding whether the testimony should only concern the narrow issue of whether the defendant has a mental disease or defect of the mind, or whether the testimony should also provide an opinion as to whether the defendant could tell right from wrong. In the M'Naghten case itself, the court permitted all of the medical experts to give testimony not only about medical facts but also legal conclusions (Finkel 1988, 19–20). Instead of restricting testimony to the defendant's mental impairment, the court permitted expert witnesses to testify as to whether the defendant could conform his behavior to the law; that is, whether he was legally insane. The judge even permitted two medical witnesses to testify who had not even examined M'Naghten; they had merely sat through the trial and observed the defendant's behavior. Both pronounced

---

FOCUS 4.3. INSANITY DEFENSE MYTHS

Michael Perlin argues that our insanity defense policies are incoherent and irrational. He contends that we based our insanity defense policies on a series of empirical and behavioral myths even though empirical research has demonstrated that these myths are false. He identifies eight separate empirical myths.

Myth #1: The insanity defense is overused.

Myth #2: Use of the insanity defense is limited to murder cases.

Myth #3: There is no risk to the defendant who pleads insanity.

Myth #4: Defendants found not guilty by reason of insanity are quickly released from custody.

Myth #5: Defendants found not guilty by reason of insanity spend much less time in custody than defendants convicted of the same offense.

Myth #6: Criminal defendants who plead insanity are usually faking.

Myth #7: Most insanity trials feature "battles of experts."

Myth #8: Criminal defense attorneys use the insanity defense plea solely to "beat the rap." (Perlin 2000, 228–30)

---

the defendant insane. However, the court's permissiveness disturbed many in the legal community who saw medical experts taking over the power of the jury by deciding issues of fact. One of questions posed to judges in the formulation of the M'Naghten rules concerned the proper role of the expert witness. The resulting rule on expert testimony stated, on the one hand, that courts should not ask medical experts for opinions about facts, for those are for the jury to decide (Finkel 1988, 21–22). However, the answer also provides a loophole, stating, "But, where the facts are admitted, or not disputed, and the question becomes substantially one of science only, it may be convenient to allow the question to be put in that general form, although the same cannot be insisted on as a matter of right" (Finkel 1988, 21).

The Durham Rule and the Ultimate Issue

As indicated earlier in this chapter, the Durham rule, or "product test" adopted by Judge Bazelon in 1954 was an attempt to bring the insanity defense in line with current psychiatric thinking. Psychiatrists would be free to inform the jury about the defendant's mental disease without confining their testimony to M'Naghten criteria. Ideally, the intent of the Durham rule was to allow the expert witness the broadest latitude to explain the defendant's symptoms and to provide a detailed clinical history of the accused so that the jury could reach a conclusion as to whether the defendant's criminal act was the product of a mental disease or defect. However, since no definition of "mental disease or defect" existed, medical experts frequently defined the term with meanings drawn from their own disciplines (Simon and Aaronson 1988, 88–90). This led to increased reliance on classifications from the *Diagnostic and Statistical Manual of Mental Disorders* of the American Psychiatric Association, which contained terms developed to aid in understanding and treating mental disorders, not in assessing criminal responsibility. The legal community became concerned with testimony that had become extremely technical. Experts could now testify about mental illnesses and their causes and consequences rather than being restricted to the issue of whether the defendant's mental illness weakened responsibility and knowledge of right from wrong. The Durham rule also blurred the line between fact and opinion (Finkel 1988, 37–39). It gave greater latitude to lawyers to ask their expert witnesses about the mental life of their client, and psychiatrists often gave conclusions about the "ultimate issue" of the defendant's state of mind at the time of the crime. In addition, the legal community criticized expert testimony under the Durham rule because psychiatry lacked the concept of an evil mind as a cause of behavior and did not frame concepts in terms of morality even though the testimony essentially expressed moral and legal conclusions.

The ALI Rule and the Ultimate Issue

As described earlier, dissatisfaction with the M'Naghten and Durham rules led to the ALI formulation of the moral penal code's test for criminal responsibility in 1962 that incorporated both cognitive and volitional tests. ALI hoped that the more explicit legal standards of this new test would remove some of the difficulties that jurors faced when deciding what weight to give to expert testimony; however, the controversy over the use of expert witnesses in the insanity trials did not end. Throughout the 1970s and into the 1980s, critics contended that expert witnesses confused the jury, hired themselves out to the highest bidder, failed to clarify the facts of a case, and generally dominated the proceedings to the detriment of an equitable resolution of the case (Simon and Aaronson 1988, 90).

The verdict in the *Hinckley* trial seemed to illustrate the dominant role often played by expert witnesses in contested insanity defense trials. In the *Hinckley* trial, expert witnesses for the defense included psychologists, psychiatrists, neuropsychiatrists, and neuroradiologists. The jurors listened to a vast amount of expert testimony from defense and prosecution experts and had to relate the testimony to an abstract concept of the insanity standard. Further, the judge instructed the jury that under the prevailing law, the government carried the burden of proof. Hinckley's acquittal not only led to Congress changing the standard for insanity in federal courts but also amending the federal rules of evidence in order to restrict mental health expert testimony. The amended rules provided that no expert witness testifying on the mental state or condition of a defendant in a criminal case "may state an opinion or inference as to whether the defendant did or did not have the mental state or condition constituting an element of the crime charged or a defense thereto. Such ultimate issues are matters for the trier of fact alone" (Opinion on Ultimate Issue, Fed. R. Evid. Rule 704[b], [2006]). This meant that the expert could not express opinions about whether the defendant was insane at the time of the crime, whether the defendant could tell right from wrong, and whether the defendant could appreciate the wrongfulness of his conduct.

Expert Testimony and the Adversary System

The limitations to expert testimony reflect the concern of legal decision makers that psychiatrists and psychologists had undue influence on ultimate legal determinations in insanity defense cases. Yet such concern fails to consider two important misconceptions. First is that those accused of crimes frequently claim insanity as their defense and are successful in their claim because of the use of expert witness testimony. The media reinforces this view by providing a great deal of publicity to high-profile insanity cases, however, research on the actual use of the insanity defense reveals that defendants rarely assert the defense and it is rarely successful when asserted. Cirincione and his colleagues reported the results of a survey of the use of the insanity defense in seven states and found that the rate of insanity pleas ranged from 0.29 to 1.73 per 100 indictments, with an average of 0.85 (less than 1 percent). The aggregated success rate for insanity pleas in that survey was 28.1 percent (Cirincione, Steadman, and McGreevy 1995). A national survey conducted by Pasewark and McGinley (1986) reported that the median success rate for insanity pleas was one acquittal for every 6.5 pleas (approximately 15 percent). Finally, Janofsky and his colleagues studied all defendants in Baltimore's circuit and district courts who asserted the insanity defense during the calendar year of 1991. They found that of the 60,432 indictments filed in the two courts, 190 defendants (0.31 per 100 indictments) entered a plea of not criminally responsible, Maryland's version of the insanity plea. All but eight defendants dropped this plea before trial, either because the defendants had their charges dropped before trial, they remained not competent to stand trial at the time of the study, or they withdrew their pleas of not criminally responsible. For the remaining eight cases, both the state and the defense agreed that the defendant was not criminally responsible, and the plea was uncontested at trial (Janofsky et al. 1996).

Second is the misconception that defendants are constitutionally entitled to use their own expert witnesses as part of their evidence to prove insanity. In *Ake v. Oklahoma* (470 U.S. 68 [1985]), the Supreme Court considered whether psychiatrists and psychologists have a legitimate role in the courtroom when the insanity defense is raised. The case concerned George Ake, a man charged with first-degree murder and shooting with intent to kill. At his arraignment, the trial court found his behavior so bizarre that the court ordered a psychiatric evaluation to determine his competency to stand trial. The psychiatrist found him incompetent to stand trial and the court committed him to a state hospital. After six weeks, the state psychiatrist found him to be competent so long as he remained on medication. At a pre-trial conference, defense counsel indicated that he would raise the insanity defense at trial and requested a psychiatric evaluation at the state's expense because the defendant was indigent. The trial court denied his motion, and the Oklahoma Court of Criminal Appeals affirmed the trial court's decision. There were no expert witnesses on either side to testify regarding the defendant's behavior at the time of the killings. The jury found him guilty and sentenced him to death.

FOCUS 4.4. THE INSANITY DEFENSE IN
OTHER COUNTRIES

Simon and Ahn-Redding (2006) studied the insanity defense in other countries. Of the twenty-two countries included in the study, only Sweden did not allow for a defense. (Sweden has legislation applicable to all mentally ill persons, including those charged with having committed criminal offenses.) Of the remaining twenty-one countries, the most commonly used criteria for determining criminal responsibility is the M'Naghten rules or a modified version of those rules. Different societies have expanded on the phrases contained in the rules. For example, traditionally the law interpreted "to know" in a narrow cognitive manner. Over time, it has come to include terms such as "unable to appreciate." In addition to M'Naghten, many of the countries studied also included a version of the irresistible impulse rule. Nine countries of the twenty-one studied employed a combination of the M'Naghten and irresistible impulse rules. Seven societies use the traditional M'Naghten rules or the more expanded version.

In almost all of the societies, a judge determines the defendant's fate. The United States involves the jury more than any of the countries included in the study. The most frequently used verdict is not guilty by reason of insanity. Only a few countries use the verdict of guilty but mentally ill. Courts in all of the countries call upon experts in psychology, psychiatry, and/or social work to examine the defendant before trial, often to determine if he or she is fit to stand trial. Courts also call upon experts during the trial to provide insight into the defendant's responsibility or lack of it for his or her criminal behavior, and after trial if a judge or jury has found the defendant not guilty by reason of insanity to advise the court about the commitment of the defendant.

In an 8 to 1 opinion, the U.S. Supreme Court reversed the Oklahoma Court of Criminal Appeals for not granting the defendant access to a psychiatric evaluation. Justice Marshall, writing for the majority, stated that where the defendant's mental condition is critical to the issue of criminal responsibility, the assistance of a psychiatrist might be crucial to the defendant's ability to marshal his defense. However, the court limited its holding to one competent psychiatrist and did not provide for a psychiatrist of the defendant's choice. Therefore, the indigent defendant is not constitutionally entitled to have more than one evaluation.

More recently, in *Clark v. Arizona* (548 U.S. 735 [2006]), the Supreme Court upheld the state's right to limit expert witnesses to show that the defendant could not form criminal intent in order to avoid juror confusion and juror misunderstanding. For more details about this case, see Focus 4.2.

THE CONTINUING DEBATE CONCERNING MORALITY, SCIENCE, AND INDIVIDUAL RESPONSIBILITY

The changes to the insanity defense doctrine and the role of the expert witness in insanity trials illustrate the uneasy connection and frequent tension between law and the behavioral sciences when punishment for wrongs committed is at issue. Perlin (2000) argues that every change in the insanity defense doctrine that reflected a greater understanding of human behavior also led to a retrenchment from what psychiatry and psychology can offer and a return to a doctrine grounded in moral/legal terms.

He claims that while overtly we search for knowledge and uni-
fying principles that would assist us in formulating a coherent
insanity defense doctrine, covertly we ignore the knowledge we
gain to maintain an underlying social vision that rejects psychological thinking and its importance in framing our standard for
blameworthiness. He contends that our society cannot accept
the proposition that psychological determinants are a valid
excuse for criminal responsibility. Instead, we rely on "ordinary
common sense" explanations grounded in medieval conceptions of free will and intentionality of the mind, in the face of
remarkable contrary evidence.

While Perlin is critical of the law's reluctance to accept
"psychological thinking," other scholars (for example, Fingarette 1972, 55–63; Finkel 1988, 327–31) claim that the thesis that law rests upon unscientific and outdated beliefs about
human nature oversimplifies the issue. This position maintains
that our society embodies certain fundamental values, in particular that normally the state shall deal with all members of
a community as responsible persons under the law. Fingarette
contends that our system of criminal law, founded as it is on the
principle of individual responsibility, is not a merely a means
toward reducing antisocial activity; the institution is itself an
essential end for the society. He argues that "we do not want
merely an orderly society; we want an order of responsible persons, responsible under the law" (Fingarette 1972, 56–57). This
line of argument implies that scientific explanations by their
nature do not assume an exalted status when compared with
the moral values of a society; rather, law uses scientific explanations in a manner appropriate to the purposes of law. Yet such
a view does not resolve the doctrinal confusion concerning
what should count as insanity that the varied state standards and
the absence of the defense in some states illustrate. This suggests that the focus should concern two issues. First, what is the
essence of insanity from a moral perspective? Second, what role

can psychiatry and psychology assume in formulating a standard that is compatible with science?

Fingarette (1972, 128–42) maintains that whether Hadfield, M'Naghten, and Yates knew what they were doing and knew what they were doing was legally wrong is beside the point. He contends that insanity is like childhood where questions of knowledge, or appreciation of what one is doing or its wrongness, or questions of voluntary action, self-control, or intent, become irrelevant. What is at issue when we call someone insane is something else, something that, among other things, renders the person non-responsible. It infects the person's will and the person's knowledge and his conduct, just as childishness qualifies a child's will, knowledge, and conduct. Some further dimension of mind is absent, a dimension that makes mere absence of compulsion or mere knowledge of what one is doing insufficient in establishing criminal responsibility. Fingarette conceptualizes insanity as the absence of *mens*. The insane individual may well be able to act voluntarily and may well formulate intentions, but something more fundamental is amiss: the lack of capacity for rational conduct concerning the criminal significance of the conduct. Insane individuals (for example, Andrea Yates) when deluded often know what is morally right and wrong in the abstract and indeed may abhor murder in general, but they dissociate the general background nexus from their particular act.

CONCLUSIONS AND IMPLICATIONS

This chapter has considered the tension between law and the behavioral sciences concerning the standard for insanity pleas and the role of the mental health community in testifying in insanity cases. This tension surfaced early on in the formulation of the insanity defense under English common law manifested in the *M'Naghten* case and continued with the formulation of insanity standards in the United States that included the irresistible impulse rule, the Durham rule, and the ALI rule.

The changes to the insanity defense standards in federal cases and in state law because of the *Hinckley* verdict signaled a retreat to a value system resting on assumptions of free will, individual responsibility, and the role of punishment in maintaining societal stability.

However, the moral claim remains confusing because of its varied definitions and the contradictory verdicts that result, as the first and second verdicts in trials of Andrea Yates illustrate. The debate between science (facts) and morality (values) continues without any promise of resolution. It is likely that high-profile insanity cases will continue to drive policy concerning what should count as insanity and what role we should give to the mental health community in insanity defense trials.

CHAPTER 5

The "Mad" or "Bad" Debate Concerning Sex Offenders

> I picked the boys because in some way they
> were the safest, the girls and the mothers
> would have been more dangerous.
> —John Geoghan*

JOHN GEOGHAN was a former Catholic priest and a convicted child molester. He was a key figure in the Roman Catholic sex abuse cases that arose in the Boston Archdiocese in the 1990s and early 2000s. More than 130 people claimed that Geoghan abused them, most when they were boys enrolled in various Boston-area parish schools. The sexual assaults began shortly after Geoghan's ordination as a priest in 1962.

The Catholic Church received complaints about Geoghan's pedophilia. Following these complaints, the Church would quietly place Geoghan on sick leave and order him to undergo psychotherapy for his pedophilic sexual impulses. After a period of treatment, psychotherapists would judge him rehabilitated, and Geoghan would then receive an assignment to another parish

---

*John Geoghan's statement during treatment sessions with Dr. Edward Messner, a psychiatrist at Massachusetts General Hospital (*Boston Globe*, January 7, 2002, http://boston.com/globe/spotlight/abuse/print/010702_geoghan.htm).

where he would return to molesting boys from families in his parish. For some thirty years, Geoghan sexually abused boys at six parishes, and for most of the time, the Archdiocese of Boston knew it. He continued to molest boys after the archdiocese removed him from parish duty and placed him in a residence for retired priests. Finally, in 1998, the Church removed him from the priesthood (Ferro 2005, 20–21).

In 1999, the state of Massachusetts indicted Geoghan on child rape charges concerning accusations of molestation of a ten-year-old-boy that took place in 1991. The trial included testimony from the victim, from a psychiatrist who treated Geoghan for his sexual fantasies about children, and from the archbishop who testified that he banned Geoghan from a swimming pool at a Boys and Girls Club after a complaint that he was having prurient conversations there. In 2002, the jury found Geoghan guilty of indecent assault and battery. The court sentenced him to nine to ten years in state prison. Courts dismissed other cases against Geoghan because the statute of limitations had run out for charging the offense. However, the Boston Archdiocese also settled civil lawsuits with other victims because of evidence that the archdiocese transferred Geoghan from parish to parish despite warnings of his behavior (Ferro 2005, 20–21).

On August 23, 2003, while in protective custody at a correctional facility, a fellow inmate, Joseph Druce, already serving a sentence of life without parole for killing a man, trapped Geoghan in his cell, strangled him, and stomped him to death. The *New York Times* reported that on January 25, 2006, the judge, following Druce's conviction at trial, sentenced him to another term of life in prison without the possibility of parole for the murder of Geoghan.

SEX OFFENDERS AND THE CRIMINAL JUSTICE SYSTEM

The issue of sexual misconduct by clergy turned out to be far bigger than the Geoghan case. The true extent of the problem became apparent when the United States Conference of Catholic Bishops released the results of a study conducted by the John Jay College of Criminal Justice in New York, which reported on the sexual abuse of minors by Catholic priests and deacons in the United States. Among its findings were accusations of sexual misconduct made against 4 percent of the 109,694 active priests in the United States from 1950 to 2002. Allegations peaked in 1980, when 800 reported cases implicated some 500 U.S. priests of alleged sexual misconduct (John Jay College of Criminal Justice 2004, 23–35).

The criminal justice system classifies as sex offenders others besides adults who sexually abuse children. For example, adults who rape other adults are categorized as sex offenders. However, a great deal of legal and behavioral science controversy concerns the degree of mental disorder in adults who sexually abuse children. These individuals often state that they are unable to control their sexual urges, as in the case of John Geoghan, who received psychiatric treatment on several occasions but who continued his sexual abuse of young boys after psychiatrists judged him rehabilitated. A major controversy for the behavioral sciences and criminal law concerns the response of the criminal justice system to the criminal behavior of these offenders given their often-admitted lack of control over their behavior. Should our policy toward these offenders reflect treatment, punishment, or both approaches?

This chapter will examine why our criminal justice system assigns criminal responsibility to sex offenders even though the system also may define them as suffering from a mental defect or mental abnormality. In presenting this issue, we will place emphasis on the special kinds of laws that exist concerning sex offenders whose victims are children and the debate about these laws. A major theme of the discussion is whether these sex offenders are "mad" or "bad" in terms of how our society should respond to their crimes. Historically, the "mad" and "bad" controversy keeps resurfacing in our policies toward sex offenders.

We will review recent controversial civil confinement laws and the U.S. Supreme Court decision concerning these laws. We will also examine the state of behavioral science research regarding treatment and rehabilitation of sex offenders and evaluate how the legal system uses the behavioral sciences to serve its purpose of incapacitation of adults who sexually abuse children.

THE ISSUE OF "MAD" OR "BAD"

Sex offenders evoke little or no sympathy from the public. Indeed, recent laws requiring community notification of the place of residence of convicted sex offenders upon release from prison reflects public outrage about brutal crimes that have been committed by sex offenders. States passed these notification laws following the arrest of a convicted child molester for the murder and rape of seven-year-old Megan Kanka in a New Jersey suburb. The media focused a great deal of attention on the crime and the fact that the offender was a previously convicted child molester who lived across the street from the victim. In 1996, President Bill Clinton signed an amendment to the Violent Crime Control and Law Enforcement Act of 1994 that required states to develop a procedure for notifying concerned people when a person convicted of certain crimes is released near their homes (Megan's Law [1996]). All fifty states have such laws although states have different procedures for making disclosures (Burdon and Gallagher 2002).

The community notification laws certainly reflect our concern about the safety of children. However, they also reflect a concern about whether sex offenders can control their behavior. At issue is whether adults who sexually molest children can be "cured," or whether upon release from prison they will once again experience the urge to molest children and, therefore, repeat their crimes. This view suggests that a mental illness or mental disorder of these offenders could explain their recidivism; in other words, they are "mad" not "bad." This debate as to whether sex offenders are mentally ill has a long history in our society.

FOCUS 5.1. SEX PREDATORS AS ENTERTAINMENT

NBC's *Dateline* TV series began a program in 2004 called "To Catch a Predator." The program has a straightforward formula. Decoys in a chat room on the Internet pretend to be thirteen- or fourteen-year-old boys or girls. They arrange to meet the "sex predator" at a home on a specified day and time. The decoy may greet the predator, but NBC correspondent Chris Hansen is inside the home and NBC films the entire encounter. When the predator leaves, police arrest him. As of March 2007, Chris Hansen had interviewed more than two hundred sexual predators that resulted in over two hundred arrests. The program is very popular but raises issues about using this approach to catch potential sex predators.

Early Sexual Psychopath Statutes

Several prominent psychiatrists, including Phillippe Pinel, James Cowles Prichard, and the father of American psychiatry, Benjamin Rush, developed the concept of the psychopathic personality during the 1800s (Patrick 2006). Each described psychopaths as persons who appeared normal, had normal intellect and an absence of psychosis, but failed to possess an adequate conscience. Thus, psychiatrists judged psychopaths unable to abide by the moral standards of society. This led a brief period during the nineteenth century that identified psychopaths as mentally ill and in need of psychiatric treatment instead of punishment. This so-called moral psychiatry movement was largely a failure since mental health professionals were unable to either cure the defective behavior or prove that it was indeed the product of a legitimate mental illness (Sabshin 1990). Nonetheless, later psychiatrists would return to the construct of psychopath in efforts to understand and describe those who appeared bereft of moral capacity and conscience.

The notion of psychopaths as mentally ill served as the basis for the sexual psychopath laws that began in the 1930s. Many states enacted "sexual psychopath" or "psychopathic personality" statutes. These statutes followed the prevailing optimism of that time, which embraced the public health model as the chief method for dealing with societal problems (Grob 1994). Moreover, the rise of the disease model of illness fundamentally changed how medicine dealt with disease. Whereas before illness was loosely understood as an imbalance of bodily fluids, called humors, the disease model proposed the idea of active transmission by pathogens (Rousseau et al. 2003). This set the stage for interventions that raised hopes that we could cure all illnesses by a heavy reliance on medicine aided by the power of the government. In terms of mental illnesses, this model prospered during the early twentieth century; however, by the end of World War II, Freudian psychoanalysis replaced the public health model for treatment of mental illnesses.

By 1960, twenty-six states and the District of Columbia had sexual psychopath laws. Under these statutes, instead of criminal incarceration, a sex offender determined to have a psychopathic personality could be civilly committed for an indefinite period under the notion that he or she suffered from a psychiatric illness amenable to treatment. The assumption of such an approach was that civil commitment was preferable to conviction and penal incarceration. Supporters of this legislation also assumed that sexual psychopaths are able to be reliably distinguished from other sex offenders and that sex offenders offend because of mental disorder or disease (Schulhofer 1996, 71–72). The emerging Freudian notion that abnormal sexual behavior was a treatable psychiatric condition and not a moral failing bolstered the idea of civil commitment for sex crimes.

The U.S. Supreme Court endorsed these laws in *Minnesota ex rel. Pearson v. Probate Court of Ramsey County* (309 U.S. 270 [1940]). In that case, Pearson challenged the constitutionality of a Minnesota statute on due process and equal protection grounds. Under the statute, the state found that Pearson was a "psychopathic personality" requiring civil commitment in lieu of criminal incarceration. Pearson appealed. The court upheld the statute against constitutional challenges in part by examining the definition of "psychopathic personality" in the Minnesota statute. The court noted the statute defined the term as "the existence in any person of such conditions of emotional instability, or impulsiveness of behavior, or lack of customary standards of good judgment, or failure to appreciate the consequences of his acts, or a combination of any such conditions, as to render such person irresponsible for his conduct with respect to sexual matters and thereby dangerous to other persons." The statute also specified that the "laws relating to insane persons or those alleged to be insane, shall apply with like force to persons having, or alleged to have, a psychopathic personality" (*Minnesota ex rel. Pearson*, 309 U.S. 272).

The Transitional Period

Although in 1940 the Supreme Court gave approval to the involuntary civil commitment of persons under "sexual psychopath" statutes in the *Minnesota ex rel. Pearson* case, starting in the late 1970s most states began to repeal the sexual predator statutes. By 1990, half of these states had repealed their statutes and most of the other states no longer made significant use of them. Several reasons account for the decline of these psychopathic personality statutes. Schulhofer (1996, 71) notes that beginning in the 1970s, a number of influential groups criticized the foundations of the statutes. In 1977, for example, the Group for the Advancement of Psychiatry formally called for the repeal of these laws, stressing that the broad definition of mental illness in sex psychopath statutes allowed almost any mental aberration or emotional disorder to qualify. Even professional medical journals carried articles criticizing the construct of sexual psychopathy as overly broad and serving legal and administrative considerations more than any true scientific understanding of sexual behavior (Bowman and Rose 1952). The repeal of the sexual psychopath statutes also coincided with the social movements of the 1960s and 1970s that questioned established authority figures. In the mental health field, authors such as Thomas Szasz (1961) and R. D. Laing (1960) questioned the basis of psychiatry and psychology as a science, claiming that both failed to demonstrate that *any* mental illnesses were in fact illnesses as conventionally conceived by medicine. Szasz and Laing asserted that mental health experts merely declared some behaviors abnormal and others normal.

While the 1960s and 1970s witnessed questioning of established authority, two other factors were taking hold that would soon change the shape the debate regarding sex offenders: sexual morality and crime. The sexual revolution of the 1960s changed popular attitudes regarding sexuality. Pervasive premarital sex, the availability of birth control and abortion, and a general openness toward sexuality were a dramatic departure from decades of sexual conservatism. However, violent crime also ballooned during the 1960s and 1970s. The homicide rate in the United States jumped from 5.1 homicides per 100,000 persons in 1960 to 9.6 per 100,000 persons in 1975 (Fox and Zawitz 2002). The overall violent crime rate increased from 160.9 incidents per 100,000 residents in 1960 to 596.6 per 100,000 residents in 1980 (Hart and Rennison 2002). Soon politicians were calling for tough prison sentences for offenders, particularly against violent offenders and drug dealers (Whitman 2003). The birth of the Internet, with its offer of anonymity and abundant supply of pornography, added to the belief that sex offenders were everywhere and children were increasingly vulnerable even in their own homes. What followed was an outcry from concerned parents and law enforcement officials seeking total incapacitation of those with the worst prurient interests.

MODERN INCAPACITATION: CRIMINAL AND CIVIL COMMITMENT

Beginning in the early 1990s, many states amended their laws to allow for civil commitment of dangerous sex offenders. What was different about these laws from their predecessors was that they provided for civil commitment of sex offenders in psychiatric hospitals *after* their prison sentences expired. Whereas in the past states sent sex offenders to state mental hospitals in lieu of imprisonment, these modern laws allowed for incarceration first and then civil commitment. In other words, under these new laws, we consider sex offenders bad *and* mad; bad because we deem their behavior worthy of prison and mad because we consider their behavior evidence of a mental abnormality requiring inpatient civil commitment. The motivation for such laws was understandable. Media accounts of prisons releasing sex offenders only to have them offend again, often against children, enraged a public who viewed the criminal justice system as too lenient on criminals.

Yet such laws are enormously controversial among legal scholars because they appear to violate a fundamental precept of American constitutional law. Under the double jeopardy and ex post facto clauses of the constitution, the government cannot punish someone twice for the same crime. To many observers, that is exactly what the new civil commitment statutes appear to do (Erickson 2001). First, the state imprisons the offender for violating the criminal code; and second, he is civilly committed, with little chance of release. Since most mental hospitals provide little or no treatment to these offenders, civil commitment appears to be merely a thinly veiled attempt to lifetime imprisonment.

In 1997, the Supreme Court decided the constitutionality of the modern civil commitment statutes in the case of *Kansas v. Hendricks* (521 U.S. 346 [1997]). Hendricks was a pedophile with a long history of sexual offenses against children. After the state of Kansas convicted him in 1994 of taking indecent liberties with two boys, the judge sentenced Hendricks to prison for ten years. After serving that sentence, he was released, but soon thereafter, the state filed a petition seeking to have him civilly committed under the state's newly amended sexually violent predator law.

In formulating the law, the Kansas legislature concluded that sexually violent predators "generally have anti-social personality features which are unamenable to existing mental illness treatment modalities and those features render them likely to engage in sexually violent behavior" (Sexually Violent Predator Act of 1994, §59–29a01). The legislature concluded that the likelihood of sexually violent predators engaging in repeat acts of predatory sexual violence is high and that the prognosis for rehabilitating sexually violent predators in a prison setting is poor. It found that this population has long-term treatment needs, and the appropriate treatment modalities are very different from the traditional treatment modalities for people committed under the general involuntary commitment statute (Sexually Violent Predator Act).

The act defined a "sexually violent predator" as "any person who has been convicted of or charged with a sexually violent offense and who suffers from a mental abnormality or personality disorder which makes the person likely to engage in the predatory acts of sexual violence" (Sexually Violent Predator Act, §59–29a02[a]). The statute did not define "personality disorder," but it defined "mental abnormality" as "a congenital or acquired condition affecting the emotional or volitional capacity which predisposes the person to commit sexually violent offenses in a degree constituting such person a menace to the health and safety of others" (Sexually Violent Predator Act, §59–29a02[b]).

Under the statute, the state found that Hendricks was a sexually violent predator and civilly committed him. At his commitment trial, Hendricks testified and admitted to a history of repeated sexual child molestation and abuse. Hendricks recognized his diagnosis as a pedophile, but he further testified that despite having received professional help for his pedophilia, he continued to harbor sexual desires for children. Hendricks admitted that he repeatedly abused children whenever he was not confined. He explained that whenever he is "stressed out," he "cannot control the urge" to molest children (*In re Care and Treatment of Hendricks,* 912 P.2d 129, 130–31 [Kan. 1996]). When he was committed, Hendricks sued and the Supreme Court agreed to hear his case.

The Supreme Court held that states are able, in certain narrow circumstances, to use civil statutes to forcibly detain people who are unable to control their behavior and thereby pose a danger to the public health and safety. A finding of dangerousness standing alone, however, is ordinarily not a sufficient ground upon which to justify involuntary commitment. The court emphasized that it had sustained civil commitment statutes when they couple proof of dangerousness with proof of some additional factor, such as "mental illness" or "mental abnormality." The court cited previous decisions in which it had upheld the involuntary civil commitment of persons for dangerousness plus an "additional factor." The factors cited by the court are "mentally retarded" (*Heller v. Doe,* 509 U.S. 312 [1993]), "mentally ill" *(Allen v. Illinois,* 478 U.S. 364 [1986]) and "psychopathic personality" (*Minnesota ex rel. Pearson v. Probate Court of Ramsey City,* 309 U.S. 270 [1940]). The court stated that these added statutory requirements served "to limit involuntary civil confinement to those who suffer from a volitional impairment rendering them dangerous beyond their control" (*Kansas v. Hendricks,* 521 U.S. 358).

The court dismissed Hendricks's argument that a "mental abnormality" is not equivalent to a "mental illness" by stating

FOCUS 5.2. SEX OFFENDERS, INVOLUNTARY CIVIL
COMMITMENT, AND PUNISHMENT

One of the issues of concern under the *modern* civil commitment statutes is whether the government is punishing a sex offender again even though the statute is a civil commitment statute. This would violate the double jeopardy and ex post facto clauses of the U.S. Constitution and provide a case for release from such confinement. In *Seling v. Young* (531 U.S. 250 [2001]), the Supreme Court considered that issue. The state of Washington had civilly committed Young under its Community Protection Act, §71.09.060 (3). The statute prohibited sexually violent predators from being placed in state mental facilities or regional rehabilitation centers. Instead, the state placed Young in a "Special Commitment Center" located within a correctional facility. Young raised the issue as to whether the statute, as applied, was punitive. Young's allegations, among others, included that he was subject to conditions more restrictive than those placed on true civil commitment detainees or even those placed on state prisoners. He also alleged that that the Special Commitment Center relied on the Department of Corrections for a host of essential services, the conditions of confinement at the Special Commitment Center are not compatible with Washington's statute's treatment purposes, and the conditions and restrictions at the Special Commitment Center are not reasonably related to a legitimate nonpunitive goal. The Supreme Court held that an involuntary commitment statute, found to be civil, could not be deemed punitive "as applied" to a single individual. Therefore, the statute was not found to violate the Constitution.

that the court, in the past, had used a variety of expressions to describe the mental condition of those properly subject to civil confinement. It noted that it had traditionally left to legislators the task of defining medical terms that have legal significance. In considering the application of the act to Hendricks, the court noted that his admitted lack of volitional control coupled with a prediction of future dangerousness adequately distinguished Hendricks from other dangerous persons who are perhaps more properly dealt with exclusively through criminal proceedings (*Kansas v. Hendricks*, 521 U.S. 359–60). The court also found that the act did not violate double jeopardy or the ex post facto clause because Hendricks was civilly confined rather than criminally incarcerated.

Mental Health Treatment of Sex Offenders

With the rise of sexual predator statutes and the increasing concern of the public for their children's safety, it is not surprising that the issue of treatment for sexual behaviors—often known as paraphilias—is a hotly contested issue. Civil commitment of sexual predators implies that there exists treatment for the mental disorder or mental abnormality linked with offending. However, understanding treatment of sex offenders relies upon how we measure success and failure. The chief measure of success in the population is recidivism, that is, how often sex offenders are arrested again for sexual offending behavior after completion of their treatment. At first blush, it appears that obtaining such information would be relatively easy: researchers could follow a group of sex offenders after they received treatment and examine criminal justice databases in the future to ascertain the rate of recidivism. However, first conceptions are often misleading, and the research on sex offenders is both complex and disappointing.

The first issue that presents itself when examining sex offenders is defining the population: who should be included under the rubric of the term sex offender? Many would argue any person who commits a sex crime should qualify, but since a variety of sexual behaviors violate the criminal code—including consensual sex between teenagers, exposing one's buttocks in public, and public urination—it becomes obvious that such a simple definition does not address most people's concerns: pedophiles and rapists. However, even a narrowed definition has problems since many criminal codes define consensual sex between teenagers as rape.

A second issue is defining recidivism. Some studies examine convictions as the measure of recidivism while others use arrests. Still others rely on offenders to self-report their own crimes. Thus, when commentators conclude that studies suggest recidivism is high (or low) for sex offenders, such conclusions are misleading since different studies measure different aspects of recidivism (Hanson and Morton-Bourgon 2005). Moreover, most researchers agree that sex offenses are generally under-reported since many victims feel ashamed or wish to protect family members who are often the perpetrators. Compounding this fact is that many studies examining recidivism only follow offenders for short periods of time (for example, five years) and thus may underestimate the true rate of recidivism over an offender's lifetime (Center for Sex Offender Management 2006; Zgoba and Simon 2005; Wollert 2006).

Despite these limitations, researchers consistently refer to one study as exemplary of research on sex offender recidivism (Prentky et al. 1997). This study examined the recidivism of all sex offenders in the state of Massachusetts from 1959 through 1985. The study showed a 19 percent recidivism rate for child molesters during a five-year follow-up period that ballooned to 52 percent during the twenty-five-year follow-up period. While initially these numbers seem large, a careful reading of the study reveals that these numbers refer to *any* criminal behavior, sexual or not. Such findings suggest that child molesters have strong antisocial tendencies and frequently break the law, but many of their crimes are not sexual in nature. Nonetheless, nearly 40 percent of child molesters were reconvicted of a sex offense during the twenty-five-year period as well as almost 50 percent of rapists. These statistics suggest that about half of sex offenders commit subsequent crimes. Advocacy groups and defense lawyers continue to argue whether this should be interpreted as a high rate or a low one.

One problem with the above study is that it examined recidivism beginning in 1959 when little treatment for sex offenders was available and was predicated on psychoanalytical notions of psychosexual development, which is largely discounted by behavioral experts today. The dominant treatment currently offered relies upon relapse prevention models and various pharmacological agents (Center for Sex Offender Management 2006). Relapse prevention was first used with alcohol and drug addicts and was born out of the cognitive-behavioral psychology movement of the 1970s. In essence, relapse prevention models focus on helping offenders identify their sexual deviance and recognize the wrongfulness of their behaviors. The most well-known model of relapse prevention is Alcoholics Anonymous and other "twelve-step" programs. The evidence is inconclusive as to whether relapse prevention works in the long term because inherently such programs require a desire for change by the offender and truthful appraisal of relapsing behavior (Marques et al. 2005; Grubin and Madsen 2006).

Another treatment strategy is the use of antidepressant medications and anti-androgen therapy. Psychiatrists use many newer antidepressants for treating obsessive-compulsive behaviors, and the medications have the notorious side effect of sexual inhibition. The idea is that such medicines can reduce obsessive thoughts about deviant sex practices while also inhibiting sexual function. Unfortunately, evidence suggests that antidepressants provide only a modest effect with sex offenders

---

FOCUS 5.3. SEX OFFENDERS AND LACK OF
CONTROL OVER DANGEROUS BEHAVIOR

In the *Kansas v. Hendricks* case discussed in the text, the
U.S. Supreme Court appeared to conclude that one of the
requirements for the involuntary civil confinement of sex
offenders was their lack of control over their dangerous
behavior. One issue for courts after the *Hendricks* decision was to determine the degree of lack of control that
would warrant such confinement. In *Kansas v. Crane* (534
U.S. 407 [2002]), the Supreme Court decided this issue.
The Kansas Supreme Court had concluded that the *Hendricks* ruling requires a finding that the defendant cannot
control his behavior and the trial court in the *Crane* case
made no such finding. The Supreme Court disagreed and
held that the *Hendricks* ruling set forth no requirement
of total or complete lack of control. However, the court
stated that the Constitution requires some lack-of-control
determination. The *Hendricks* ruling therefore requires
an abnormality or disorder that makes it difficult, if not
impossible, for the person to control his behavior.

---

because deviant sexual interests are not wholly obsession based
but probably rooted in deviant behavior in itself (Land 1995).
Moreover, the offender must be trusted to take these medicines
daily, and there are no reliable tests to ascertain whether, in fact,
they take the medicine as prescribed.

Anti-androgen therapy is also a popular treatment with sex
offenders (Prentky 1997). These treatments lower testosterone
levels below detectable limits under the theory that testosterone is required for sex drive. Anti-androgen therapies are very
expensive and provide a host of ethical questions since long-term

FOCUS 5.4. LEROY HENDRICKS'S RELEASE FROM CIVIL COMMITMENT

One of the issues that sex offenders face is finding a place to live after they are released from prison or civil commitment. State laws require sex offender registration and community notification—indeed, residents can use the Internet to find out if sex offenders are living in their community—which can make it difficult for offenders to find housing. Leroy Hendricks faced such a situation. Under phase 6 of the Kansas Sexually Violent Predator Act, Hendricks successfully applied for transition to conditional independent living. Existing transitional housing set up for sexually violent predators able to reenter the workforce when released was not appropriate for Hendricks because he had several physical impairments resulting from a stroke and diabetes, in addition to his diagnosis of pedophilia. At the time of his conditional release, Hendricks was seventy-one years old. His destination was to be a newly created group home for sexually violent predators in rural Leavenworth County, Kansas. The county sued, claiming that the owners of the group home failed to obtain a special use permit as required under law. The county asked for and obtained a temporary restraining order. Hendricks was transferred to a state hospital where he remained throughout subsequent litigation. See *Board of County Commissioners v. Whitson*, 132 P. 3d 920 (Kan. 2006).

reductions of testosterone profoundly affect the body and are associated with numerous health issues, including osteoporosis. Moreover, evidence suggests that even substantially reducing testosterone does not always eliminate the offending behaviors since penile erection is not required to sexually abuse another person. Reports of sexual recidivism among offenders receiving anti-androgen therapy once again suggest that the deviant sexual behavior is not exclusively based on biological sexual arousal but in the deviance itself. While some feminist theories suggest the deviance lies within the power differential between the offender and the victim (L. Walker 2006), the evidence suggests that this holds true for only some offenders and not others. Indeed, there appears to be much heterogeneity among sex offenders, and consequently, varied treatment approaches are likely needed depending on the particular offender.

Arriving at meaningful treatments for sex offenders is slow, especially given the politics seen frequently with this population. Despite the numerous claims that sex offenders represent a clear danger to women and children, little public funding is available in the United States for scientists wishing to find more effective treatment. The National Institutes of Health rarely fund research because sexual offending behavior is considered criminal in our culture. The Department of Justice rarely funds such research, viewing behavior as within the domain of mental health. The result of these contradictory policies is that we spend little money beyond mere confinement of sex offenders either in prison or under the modern civil confinement laws.

CONCLUSION: CIVIL CONFINEMENT OF SEXUAL PREDATORS AND THE BEHAVIORAL SCIENCES

A central theme of sex offender statutes is their claim to validity because of the presence of behavioral science and medicine in the statutes (Janus 1999). The claim that sexual predators have psychopathic personalities or mental abnormalities makes it appear that agreement exists among professionals concerning the reasons for sexual predator offending. Moreover, including such behavioral science and medical terminology also makes it seem that we have reduced legal issues of social and moral values to questions of science. That is hardly the case. However, the sexual predator laws and court decisions frame the central points of the dispute as questions of science rather than of values. In *Kansas v. Hendricks,* the court appeared to claim that science is competent to make the discriminations critical to the legitimacy of the laws. In sum, the sexual predator laws and the court's opinion use science to further incapacitate those sex offenders viewed as a threat to children.

The use of science to legitimize these statutes is problematic because the approach of science conflicts with the approach used by law. Moreover, as discussions of competency and the insanity defense demonstrate, criminal law is not consistent in its use of behavioral science and medicine. Clearly, the Durham rule for insanity fell from grace in the 1960s because it contained too much room for scientific and behavioral science intrusion into the world of law. Janus (1999, 351–67) argues that by ignoring the legal issues, law gives too much power to science so that the methods and categories of science come to dominate the nonscientific values and viewpoints of law. For example, we consider "disorders" and "dangerousness" as naturally existing categories rather than as socially defined and hence arbitrary and contingent constructs. Furthermore, as we have discussed throughout this book, it is important to consider that the position of science is one of determinism in which behavior is more or less "constrained" or "limited" by biological or environmental causes. This position stands in marked contrast to a legal system in which the concept of "free will" forms one of its basic assumptions. How does one consider the situation in *Hendricks*, given the legal and the behavioral science concepts used in sexual predator statutes and the use of both criminal and civil confinement? Did Hendricks both "choose" to molest children *and* have a mental abnormality, in which he lacked volitional control over his behavior? A system that operates under both viewpoints at the same time is not a moral one.

As the discussion of the sexual psychopath statutes of the 1930s indicates, mental "illnesses," "defects," or "abnormalities" that result in an inability to control behavior are problematic categories in criminal law. Persons whose criminal conduct arises from "volitional impairment" due to a mental state that renders them "dangerous beyond their control" represent a category of persons that pose a dilemma for us in terms of our social and moral valuing of free will or choice.

CHAPTER 6

Juvenile Offenders, Developmental Competency, and Mental Illness

> I don't know what's wrong with me. . . . My head just doesn't work right. . . . I had no other choice. . . . Oh, my god, my parents were good people, I'm just so fucked up in the head, . . . God damn it . . . these voices inside my head. . . . I had no other choice. It was the only thing I could do.
>
> —Kip Kinkel*

ON MAY 20, 1998, at the age of fifteen, Kip Kinkel killed his parents in their home. The next day he walked into his high school cafeteria and sprayed students with fifty rounds from a semiautomatic rifle, killing two students and wounding twenty-five others. Although Kinkel was fifteen, the state of Oregon prosecuted him as an adult. Three days before trial, Kinkel accepted

---

*Excerpts from Kip Kinkel's full interview with Detective Al Warthen at the Springfield, Oregon, police station, conducted on the morning of May 21, 1998, two hours after he opened fire on the Thurston High School cafeteria and the day after he murdered his parents (*Frontline*, "The Killer at Thurston High" that aired on January 8, 2000; a transcript of the story and the confession is located at http://www.pbs.org/wgbh/pages/frontline/shows/kinkel/).

a plea agreement and therefore abandoned the possibility of an acquittal based on a defense of insanity. The judge sentenced him to more than 111 years in prison, without any chance of parole.

The judge handed down this sentence after a hearing in which he listened to testimony about Kinkel's mental health. The defense called a number of expert witnesses in an effort to prove that Kinkel was mentally ill. Psychologists testified that Kinkel suffered from a psychotic disorder with major paranoid symptoms, potentially a form of early onset schizophrenia. They also testified that at the time of the killings Kinkel was under the influence of auditory hallucinations. The defense presented evidence of a history of mental illness, including schizophrenia in Kinkel's extended family. A pediatric neurologist testified that Kinkel's brain showed "holes" in areas of the frontal lobe, the area associated with emotional control and decision making. He testified that new research indicated that children who had this reduced brain activity could later develop schizophrenia. However, the testimony of defense experts did not affect the judge's decision concerning Kinkel's sentence. Rather, the judge began the sentencing hearing by citing a 1996 change to the Oregon constitution, which shifted the focus of criminal punishment from the principles of reformation to the protection of society and personal accountability.

On appeal, Kinkel's attorneys argued that given his mental illness, his sentence violated the Oregon constitution because the trial judge placed more emphasis on the protection of society than on reformation. They also argued that Kinkel's sentences, when viewed together, violated the section of the Oregon constitution that prohibited cruel and unusual punishment. The appellate court, however, disagreed and affirmed Kinkel's sentence (*Oregon v. Kinkel,* 56 P. 3d 463 [Ore. Ct. App. 2002]).

THE KINKEL CASE IN CONTEXT: TWO POLICY ISSUES

Why did the judge decide to sentence Kinkel to a life sentence without the possibility of parole even though his defense counsel presented a great deal of evidence concerning Kinkel's mental illness? Moreover, why did the state of Oregon prosecute Kinkel as an adult and sentence him as an adult even though he was mentally ill and only fifteen at the time of the shootings? How do such policies fit with research in the behavioral sciences concerning the cognitive and emotional development of children and adolescents?

Our discussion of the colliding perspectives of criminal law and the behavioral sciences continues when viewing these two perspectives on the criminal culpability of youthful offenders. As discussed in previous chapters, our system of criminal law rests upon an assumption of free will. We assign criminal responsibility, with narrow exceptions, based on a belief that regardless of environment or personal history, the individual could have chosen not to commit the criminal act. This perspective stands in marked contrast to empirical findings in the behavioral sciences that biological, psychological, and social factors explain behaviors associated with criminal conduct. These factors may impair or negate an individual's ability to exercise choice. Nowhere are the contradictory perspectives of criminal law and the behavioral sciences more evident than in the case of child and adolescent offenders.

The Kip Kinkel case dramatically illustrates these colliding perspectives in two respects that form the major themes of this chapter: changes in attitudes toward juvenile offenders and skepticism toward mental illness as a cause of criminal behavior, whatever the age of the perpetrator. Historically, our policies concerning how to treat youth who commit crimes demonstrate shifting views about youth's criminal culpability. Since the 1970s, policies in the United States have increasingly reflected the belief that children and adolescents are just like adults in terms of their criminal culpability; therefore, we should punish them for their crimes. This attitude stands in marked contrast with earlier ones that viewed youth as morally immature and

FOCUS 6.1. KIP KINKEL'S WRITINGS AND CONFESSION

Police took custody of Kip Kinkel at Thurston High School. At the police station, Kip told police he had also killed his parents. When police arrived at the Kinkel home, the soundtrack to the movie *Romeo and Juliet* was in the CD player, set to continuous play. Police found the bodies of both parents. They also found a large collection of knives and guns, various books and documents on making explosives, numerous improvised explosive devices, and ingredients for making explosive devices. A handwritten note lay on the coffee table:

> I have just killed my parents! I don't know what is happening. I love my mom and dad so much. I just got two felonies on my record. My parents can't take that! It would destroy them. The embarrassment would be too much for them. They couldn't live with themselves. I'm so sorry. I am a horrible son. I wish I had been aborted. I destroy everything I touch. I can't eat. I can't sleep. I didn't deserve them. They were wonderful people. It's not their fault or the fault of any person, organization or television show. My head just doesn't work right. God damn these VOICES inside my head. I want to die. I want to be gone. But I have to kill people. I don't know why. I am so sorry! Why did God do this to me. I have never been happy. I wish I was happy. I wish I made my mother proud. I am nothing! I tried so hard to find happiness. But you know me I hate everything. I have no other choice. What have I become? I am so sorry.

Later in the day following the shootings, Kinkel gave a lengthy confession in a tape-recorded interview to Detective Al Warthen at the police station. He was able to remember his actions just prior, during, and immediately after the shootings, including the fact that his father was angry with him because police had found a gun in Kinkel's locker at school. However, although he was able to remember the details surrounding his actions at the shootings, Kinkel stated several times during the course of his confession that he "had no other choice." Near the conclusion of the interview, the following exchange took place between Detective Warthen and Kinkel:

AW: I think that it goes without saying at least from my perspective but maybe . . . I want to hear it from your perspective, did you know it was wrong to shoot your dad, your mom, and the kids at school?

KK: I had no other choice. It was the only thing I could do.

AW: What were the other choices that you didn't have a choice of?

KK: I didn't know. I couldn't think, I couldn't do anything.

AW: If your dad hadn't talked to you the way he did, would that have changed the outcome?

KK: I don't know.

———

Adapted from *Frontline*, "The Killer at Thurston High," January 8, 2000. A complete transcript of Kip's confession is at http://www.pbs.org/wgbh/pages/frontline/shows/kinkel/.

led to the formation of the juvenile court movement. The current policy of treating youths like adults fails to consider current behavioral science research that demonstrates that the capacity for understanding, reasoning, and decision making changes as a young person becomes older. In fact, research suggests that the frontal lobes of the brain do not finish developing until the late twenties. But rather than formulating a conception of blameworthiness that considers behavioral science research, our current policy increasingly blurs the differences between children and adults.

In addition, when adolescents with mental disorders commit crimes, the public, grounded in a simplified belief in free will, is as likely to be as skeptical of claims such as insanity as they are with adults. Consequently, seriously mentally ill adolescent offenders find themselves criminalized in much the same way as mentally ill adult offenders. Moreover, like adults with mental illnesses, lack of available and proper treatment in their communities leaves juveniles more vulnerable to committing crimes; once they are sentenced to juvenile or adult correctional facilities, they face the same lack of treatment issues as adults. Indeed, as we will describe more fully in this chapter, recent research demonstrates that the use of juvenile detention facilities as well as prisons to house children and adolescents with mental disorders is widespread and is a serious national problem.

Interpretations of juvenile culpability have shifted throughout history: conceptions of free will clash with interpretations grounded in a deterministic framework. Recent research in the behavioral sciences that challenges the increasingly frequent policy of treating juveniles like adults in terms of their blameworthiness. Instead, developmental psychology offers empirical research that examines the role of psychological immaturity in youth decision making. Treating juvenile offenders like adults creates particular problems for youths who have mental illnesses.

YOUTH AND CRIMINAL CULPABILITY:
SHIFTING LEGAL DEFINITIONS AND PROCEDURES

In order to evaluate critically our present policies concerning mentally ill juvenile offenders, it is useful to examine the criminal culpability of youth from a historical perspective. Viewing the legal system from such a perspective enables us to understand the social context in which policies emerge and change over time and reveals shifting views concerning criminal culpability or blameworthiness. These shifting views do not reflect a linear progression of our knowledge concerning the moral blameworthiness of youths; rather, criminal law's perception reflects changes in public and political sentiment concerning the youth who commit crimes.

Common Law, Free Will, and the Infancy Defense

In chapter 1, we discussed the importance of English common law to our American criminal justice system in terms of how the assumption of free will, the cornerstone of our criminal justice system, is rooted in English common law. There the idea developed that the legal system should only hold criminally responsible those persons who are able to exercise free will, in other words, those who chose their actions. Before the development this idea, only commission of a wrongful act *(actus reus)* was necessary in order to find a defendant guilty of a crime. Eventually, however, judges developed the idea that culpability for a crime should entail the presence of a guilty mind *(mens rea)* in addition to the wrongful act. This change occurred because of the influence of ecclesiastical law on secular law. Ecclesiastical law concerned itself with culpability for sin, based on the ability to distinguish between what the Bible considered good or evil. Secular law gradually developed this ecclesiastical idea of criminal culpability. So English common law held that we should not treat an insane defendant as a responsible moral agent even though he committed a criminal act: under the common law view of criminal culpability, one did not punish the insane because they could not understand the moral implications of their acts. Society reserved punishment for individuals who could make choices. The insane were unlike other individuals, who were considered to be endowed by nature with equal ability, as free and responsible moral agents, at liberty to obey or disobey the law.

HALE, BLACKSTONE, AND THE INFANCY DEFENSE. English common law also gradually developed the idea that we should not treat children as criminally culpable and hold them legally responsible for criminal acts because they also lacked the capacity to know wrongfulness; therefore, they could not exercise free will and form criminal intent. First articulated by Sir Matthew Hale (1736/2003), the lord chief justice of the King's Bench in England from 1671 to 1676, this defense constituted a series of presumptions concerning a child's capacity to take responsibility for acts. Hale defined infants as persons under the age of eighteen and then subdivided them into four categories that correlated degree of legal responsibility with age level. He assigned or withheld legal accountability for criminal activity according to whether or not the child was *doli capax*—possessed of the intelligence and comprehension to form the blameworthy intent necessary for the commission of a crime.

Under the age-based system of classification developed by Hale, children under seven were termed *infantia,* by definition *doli incapax* (incapable of malice) and barred from prosecution. Between the ages of seven and eleven, children occupied an in-between stage. They were not yet designated *actas pubertati proxima,* the age of criminal responsibility, but were no longer infants. Children within this age bracket were still subject to the legal presumption of incapacity, but the state could rebut that presumption. Youths aged twelve to fourteen were likewise presumptively *doli incapax,* but they were attributed greater physical and emotional maturity that rendered the presumption much weaker. At fourteen years of age, the law considered a youth sufficiently mature to formulate a criminal intent and incur criminal liability for their actions (Hale 1736/2003, 16–28).

Sir William Blackstone, who served as a judge on the English Court of Common Pleas nearly a century later, modified Hale's twofold requirement to a single criterion, which he termed "a defect of understanding" (Blackstone 1769/1979, 21). Blackstone argued that a defect of understanding applied not only to the case of infancy but also to "idiots" and "lunatics" as well as to persons who are intoxicated at the time of the criminal act. In these cases, Blackstone posited that the individual had a deficiency in will that excused the person from the "guilt of crimes" because the "will does not join with the act" and "an unwarrantable act without a vicious will is no crime at all." He further explained, "For where there is no discernment, there is no choice; and where there is no choice, there can be no act of the will, which is nothing else but a determination of one's choice, to do or to abstain from a particular action: he therefore, that has no understanding, can have no will to guide his conduct" (21).

Blackstone, like Hale, believed that the law should consider a young person's criminal culpability in terms of the youth's understanding and judgment rather than simply in terms of the chronological age of the child. Both Hale and Blackstone believed that it was moral discrimination as well as appreciation of consequences that defined a child's criminal culpability. From their perspective, culpability meant the child's capacity to discern the difference between good and evil. They both agreed that the evidence of "malice" or "vicious will" ought to be strong and clear beyond all doubt and contradiction.

THE INFANCY DEFENSE IN AMERICA. In the American colonies, children younger than twelve faced criminal prosecutions in adult criminal courts involving procedures identical to those used to try adults; however, they could assert the infancy defense and request that the court excuse them from responsibility for their actions. For example, the laws of Massachusetts passed in 1641 contained this provision concerning children:

Tryals
4. Also Children, Ideots, Distracted persons, and all that are Strangers or new comers to our Plantation, shall have such allowances, and dispensations in any case, whether Criminal or others, as Religion and Reason require. (Sanders 1970, 317)

Asserting the infancy defense did not guarantee that the court would excuse children from responsibility. Using the categories and assumptions developed by Hale and Blackstone, courts could find children above the age of seven criminally culpable for their acts. Once convicted, young offenders faced a full range of penalties that could include corporal punishment as well as incarceration. In the American colonies, moreover, courts ordered the execution of some children as young as ten years old (Sanders 1970, 317–42).

By the eighteenth century, American criminal law also reflected the principles of the classical school of criminology associated particularly with the work of Cesare Beccaria. The classical school offered a system of impartial and impersonal justice that matched the severity of the punishment to the severity of the crime. Beccaria believed that nature endowed individuals with equal ability; that individuals were free and responsible moral agents who could choose to do right or wrong and should, therefore, enjoy or suffer the consequences of their actions. Criminal behavior was the result of the moral failing of the individual. The law need only express how repugnant a given crime was to society and apply a penalty that matched it in seriousness. While youth accused of crimes continued to assert the infancy defense, those convicted faced punishment based on the principles of the classical school (Beccaria 1963).

FOCUS 6.2. BLACKSTONE ON THE CRIMINAL
RESPONSIBILITY OF CHILDREN

But by the law, as it now stands, and has stood at least
ever since Edward the Third, the capacity of doing ill, or
contracting guilt, is not so much measured by years and
days, as by the strength of the delinquent's understanding
and judgment. For one lad of eleven years old may have as
much cunning as another of fourteen; and in these cases
our maxim is, "malitia supplet aetatem." Under seven
years of age, indeed, an infant cannot be guilty of a felony.
Also, under fourteen, though an infant shall be "prima
facie" adjudged to be "doli incapax;" yet if it appear to
the court and jury that he was "doli capax," and could
discern between good and evil, he may be convicted and
suffer death. Thus a girl of thirteen has been burnt for
killing her mistress: and one boy of ten, been sentenced
to death, and he of ten years actually hanged; because it
appeared upon their trials, that the one hid himself, and
the other hid the body he had killed, which hiding manifested a consciousness of guilt, and a discretion to discern
good and evil. And there was an instance in the last century where a boy of eight years old was tried at Abingdon
for firing two barns; and it appearing that he had malice,
revenge, and cunning, he was found guilty, condemned,
and hanged accordingly. . . . But, in all such cases, the
evidence of that malice which is to supply age, ought to
be strong and clear beyond all doubt and contradiction.
(Blackstone 1769/1979, 23–24)

Juvenile Courts, Parens Patriae, and Moral Immaturity

In the late nineteenth century, social reformers in America, primarily those involved in the Progressive movement, argued for the creation of a new and separate court to resolve legal problems concerning dependent, neglected, and delinquent youth. These social reformers were concerned with many different social problems concerning youth that were associated with industrialization in America, including the employment of children in the labor market and the methods that the state used to address crimes and other deviant behavior committed by young people. In particular, they observed that although very young children could successfully assert the infancy defense, this option was frequently not available for older children. They questioned the wisdom of exposing these youthful offenders to adult trials, convictions, and prison sentences in the company of hardened criminals. The approach advanced by the Progressives was the creation of a juvenile court separate from adult criminal court because children—even children who broke the law—differed from adults. They argued that youth, as an offender class, lacked social and moral training. The state, acting through the juvenile court, should treat them not as responsible moral agents subject to the condemnation of the community but as wards of the state in need of care. Idealistically, these reformers believed that a special court for youth could diagnose and prevent as well as cure delinquency.

In her historical analysis of the juvenile court movement, Ryerson (1978) explains that a new "positivist school" of criminology developed in the last quarter of the nineteenth century that aimed toward the elimination of crime through the application of the scientific method. The Progressives found intellectual support for their interpretation of delinquent behavior and the need for a separate justice system for youth from the "positivist school" of criminology. Positivists challenged the notion that the singular cause of crime resided in the free moral choice of the criminal and, instead, considered criminals to be constrained by forces beyond their control. Moreover, they argued that science could empirically demonstrate these causes of criminal behavior. By suggesting that criminals were constrained or guided in their choices by forces beyond their control, the positivist school of criminology was also suggesting that punishment was a senseless means of dealing with criminals. In addition, by stating that there were several possible causes of criminal behavior, positivists focused on the offender as well as the offense. The positivist view "demanded consideration of each criminal's background and personal traits as part of an intelligent disposition; it demanded a system of individualized justice in which punishment and deterrence were of limited relevance" (Ryerson 1978, 22).

The view of forces beyond the criminal's control became the model of criminal behavior in the period that produced the juvenile court. The environmental facts of industrialization and urbanization dominated the explanations of juvenile crime. The real cause of juvenile crime, positivists argued, was poverty in the urban setting and the effects of poverty on morality. Positivists articulated this relationship between poverty and juvenile crime:

> slum parents did not give their children sufficient social and moral training. Through overexposure, even upstanding slum parents became hardened and accustomed to immoral and criminal people around them and failed to combat their influence on the children. Since children learned primarily through imitation, their futures depended on the examples they found in their environment. Thus, the environmentalist wing of the "positivist school" put the burden of responsibility on society: economic and social systems produced citizens who were physically and morally unfit for social life, and adults ill equipped or disinclined to raise children properly. (Ryerson 1978, 25)

Progressives used the theories of the positivists and blamed society for individual malfunction. While the free will interpretation viewed human failings as the cause of crime, Progressives reversed the causal chain and saw social ills as the cause rather than the result of a defective character. However, if the social context rather than individual human failing was responsible, then the social context should be the focus of change. By manipulating the environment in which people lived, Progressives believed that society could instill the qualities that permitted humane and orderly social life.

In addition, in the late nineteenth and early twentieth centuries, psychologists, urban reformers, and educators developed the concept of adolescence as a specific stage in the life cycle. In his discussion of adolescence, Kett (1977) describes how during this period of time, society no longer viewed young people as troublesome, the quality traditionally associated with youth. Instead, society saw them as vulnerable, passive, awkward, and malleable. This research also emphasized that antisocial behavior was not the fault of children themselves but rather the result of a harsh social environment. Educators and psychologists advocated a constructive, nonpunitive approach to juvenile misbehavior, which concentrated on providing a healthy, respectable environment that could guide the unfolding of a moral adult (Kett 1977, 215–44).

The founders of the juvenile court used developments in criminology and psychology as the rationale for a separate court for youth. Both positivism and the belief in adolescent malleability found in the psychological and counseling literature were powerful forces that shaped juvenile policy during the last quarter of the nineteenth century and the first half of the twentieth century. Reformers assumed that within each young person was the potential and the desire to be an upstanding citizen and what was needed was the example of persons of good moral character to transform that potential into reality (Ryerson 1978, 25–34). The model of the criminal, and therefore the youthful offender, as a free moral agent was dismissed in favor of a model

FOCUS 6.3. POSITIVISM AND THE CRIMINAL
RESPONSIBILITY OF CHILDREN

A book on child development published in 1898 explained
the limitations on free moral choice in the following way:
"One is most apt to think of his freedom as permission
to exercise himself within the demarcations set up by his
environment; or one might compare it to the freedom
which a prisoner, bound hand and foot, has to contract
his muscles. In spite of such freedom he is still bound.
And actually a member of a civilized community is bound
physically, mentally, and spiritually. He can no more be
said to have real liberty of choice than a bird in a cage"
(Oppenheim 1908, 4).

of the youthful offender as compelled by social forces to disobey
the law and capable of being rehabilitated by altering the environment to shape moral, law-abiding behavior.

Reformers created the juvenile court as a wholly distinct
court from criminal court in form, procedure, and purpose. The
theory of juvenile court was rooted in a social welfare philosophy with the goal of rehabilitation of the youthful offender.
Since the purpose of juvenile court was rehabilitation, it was
structured as a civil, informal, and nonadversarial proceeding;
the state proceeded as *parens patriae*, that is, as a legal guardian
to the youth. Its objectives were to determine the needs of the
child and of society rather than adjudicating criminal conduct. A
cardinal rule of the juvenile court movement was that the youth
should receive, whenever possible, needed rehabilitation in a
home—either the child's home or someone else's—rather than
in an institution. The therapeutic approach of juvenile courts
precluded attempts to raise the infancy defense because *parens*

patriae theory depends on the notion that the youthful offender is being helped and is not being tried for a crime and punished as a criminal.

Viewing Young Offenders as Adults

Several decades after the creation of the juvenile court, legal practitioners and child advocates raised concerns about the broad discretion given to juvenile court judges. Critics argued that youth were virtually powerless to contest whatever length and kind of rehabilitation the court sought to impose. Indeed, judges often sentenced youthful offenders to reformatories or "industrial schools" rather than following the Progressive ideal of rehabilitation in a home environment. Furthermore, judges could sentence youthful offenders for lengths of time that far outlasted the harshest sentence they could have received upon conviction in adult criminal court. Beginning in the 1960s, a concerned Supreme Court issued a series of decisions granting many constitutional rights to minors involved in juvenile court proceedings previously reserved only for adults. Two decisions are especially noteworthy. In the landmark case of *In re Gault* (387 U.S. 1 [1967]), the court reconceived juvenile court procedures. It declared that minor children had constitutional rights to notice, counsel, confront witnesses, cross-examination, and against self-incrimination. *In re Winship* (397 U.S. 358 [1970]) is perhaps the most significant decision in the erosion of the doctrine of *parens patriae*. In *Winship,* the court found that due process required the application of the criminal standard of proof beyond a reasonable doubt. The court stated that the "same considerations that demand extreme caution in fact-finding to protect the innocent adult apply as well to the innocent child" (*In re Winship,* 397 U.S. 365).

While initial changes to procedures of juvenile court were in the interests of increasing the protections available to children, they came with a shifting view of youth's criminal culpability. By extending adult constitutional protections to juvenile proceedings, juvenile courts began to view adolescents as more like adults than like children. Juvenile courts viewed young offenders as having some responsibility for criminal acts, as having sufficient moral judgment to justify punishment. However, in the 1960s and early 1970s, the legal system still viewed adolescents as having diminished responsibility because of immaturity and because of youth's lessened capacity and experience with self control. Zimring's research on the sentencing policy toward young offenders indicates that juvenile courts saw the criminal choices of adolescents as less culpable and thus as deserving less punishment than those of adults. The goal of intervention with adolescents through the juvenile justice system was to teach lessons in accountability as preparation for adulthood (Zimring 1978, 88–96).

In the late 1980s, another shift in public opinion occurred, rejecting the assumption of moral immaturity in children and the rehabilitative approach that provided the rationale for the juvenile court. This shift in sentiment occurred because media accounts as well as Justice Department statistics reported an increase in homicides and aggravated assaults committed by youths. These cases captured the attention of the public as well as of policy makers. Explanations for the increase in lethal violence by youth ranged from the availability of guns and drug trafficking by youth to notions that our society had spawned a new generation of "super-predators." In *Body Count: Moral Poverty . . . and How to Win America's War against Crime and Drugs,* Bennett, DiIulio, and Walters (1996, 27) argued that "super-predators" were radically impulsive, brutally remorseless children driven to commit acts with full awareness of and indifference to the wrongfulness and consequences of such behavior. While commentators and policy makers typically used the "super-predator" label to describe violent teenagers, they also used the term to apply to preadolescent offenders, cases involving children under twelve years old. Thus, the notion of free will surfaced again in

---

FOCUS 6.4. CHILDREN OR SUPER-PREDATORS?

Consider the following profile of super-predators: they are "radically impulsive, brutally remorseless youngsters . . . who murder, assault, rape, rob, burglarize, deal deadly drugs, join gun-toting gangs, and create serious communal disorders. They do not fear the stigma of arrest, the pains of imprisonment, or the pangs of conscience. They perceive hardly any relationship between doing right (or wrong) now and being rewarded (or punished) for it later. To these mean-street youngsters, the words 'right' and 'wrong' have no fixed meaning" (Bennett, DiIulio, and Walters 1996, 27).

---

the manner in which society explained crimes committed by children and adolescents.

Zimring (1998) indicates that the term "super-predator" presented a new image to the public, far removed from that of the adolescent image of the juvenile court era. The super-predator image disassociated the policies toward young offenders from other policies toward youth that society based on youthful immaturity, such as the age for drinking alcohol. Renaming the class "super-predators" had a connotation quite distant from terms like "child," "youth," "adolescent," and "kid" and resulted in a shift in public attitude toward young offenders. Juvenile justice policy reflected the shift in public sentiment. Two of the consequences were the incarceration of youthful offenders for longer periods when sentenced by juvenile court and the enactment of broader waiver provisions to facilitate transfer of violent juveniles for trial as adult offenders. In both situations, the criminal justice system and the juvenile justice system emphasized safety, punishment, and individualized responsibility rather than the rehabilitative philosophy that had been the cornerstone of the juvenile justice system.

BEHAVIORAL SCIENCE RESEARCH: YOUTH AND THE DEVELOPMENT OF BLAMEWORTHINESS

While current justice policy increasingly treats youthful offenders like their adult counterparts, a very different view of the criminal culpability of youthful offenders emerges from behavioral science research, especially research in developmental psychology. Behavioral science research does not use the concept of free will to explain youthful offending. Rather, behavioral science examines how fundamental psychological and intellectual requirements for criminal culpability gradually develop during childhood and adolescence. Rather than viewing youthful offenders as indistinguishable from adults in terms of blameworthiness, this research analyzes how adolescent involvement in crime differs from that of adults in ways that are important to assessments of culpability. More specifically, behavioral science research considers (1) the role of developmental factors in youthful offending, (2) the impact of developmental immaturity on trial competency, and (3) the effects of mental disorder on developmental immaturity.

The Role of Developmental Factors in Youthful Offending

In recent years, behavioral science research has enhanced our understanding of the role of developmental factors in youthful offending in two important dimensions that serve to distinguish the criminal culpability of youths from adults. First, there are developmental influences on decision making that may distinguish the choices of adolescents from those of adults. Second, this research clarifies the role that youthful offending may play in adolescence. It indicates that many youths engage in criminal behavior during adolescence but do not continue to engage in criminal behavior as adults. These developmental factors would

seem to call for a different standard for assessing the blameworthiness of youthful offenders—one that would take into account
developmental immaturity.

DEVELOPMENTAL INFLUENCES ON DECISION MAKING. Several
psychologists and legal scholars have reviewed the research findings concerning developmental influences on decision making
(Scott and Grisso 1997, 2005; Scott and Steinberg 2003; Grisso
and Schwartz 2000; Steinberg and Cauffman 1996; Steinberg
2005) and have reached two conclusions. First, on average,
youths tend not to have adult-like capacities for understanding
and reasoning until sometime in early to mid-adolescence. Second, achieving those capacities does not mean that adolescents
can necessarily employ them with the efficiency or dependabil-
ity that one associates with adult performance. More specifically,
Scott and Grisso (2005, 812–17) identify four spheres of development—neurological, intellectual, emotional, and psychosocial—that affect the capacities of individuals to understand information and make decisions. Recent developmental research
concerning youth development in these four spheres confirms
that youth are in the process of developing adult capacities, but
they have not attained adult maturity.

- Neurological Development. Neuroscience research on
  brain development probes the biological basis of psychological development. Only in the past decade have scientists
  learned that brain development continues through adolescence. This neurological development is especially evident
  in the early adolescent years, although it continues more
  slowly through middle adolescence. One of the last areas of
  the brain to develop is the prefrontal cortex, which functions as a center for "executive cognitive functions" such as
  planning, organizing information, and thinking about possible consequences of action. Another important function

of the prefrontal cortex is "affect regulation"—the capacity to inhibit or delay impulsive and emotional reactions sufficiently to allow for rational consideration of appropriate responses. Development of the prefrontal cortex and of connections from it to other regions of the brain continues through adolescence. This research suggests that youths in early and mid-adolescence generally are neurologically immature. Their brains are "unstable"; they have not yet attained their adult neurological potential to respond effectively to situations that require careful or reasoned decisions, and they may be more inclined than adults to act impulsively and without planning.

■ Intellectual Development. Cognitive development during adolescence has been the focus of scientific interest for many years. Intellectual capacities increase in childhood and into adolescence. Although there is much variability among individuals, children and younger teens differ significantly from adults in their cognitive functioning. In part, this is simply because adults have experience that is more extensive. As youths proceed through adolescence, they acquire new information through experience and education, and "practice" their cognitive abilities in a broader range of contexts. Beyond the accumulation of knowledge and experience, intellectual development in adolescence also involves improvements in basic information processing skills including organization, attention, and short- and long-term memory. Gains in deductive reasoning and abstract thinking, including the ability to think about hypothetical situations and consider that others have perspectives different from one's own, characterize early adolescence. By mid-adolescence, evidence suggests that capacities for reasoning and understanding may roughly approximate that of adults. However, little research has examined adolescent decision making in stressful and unstructured situations.

- Emotional Development. Youths and adults also differ in their capacity for impulse control—the ability to delay response in situations in which emotional arousal is high. Impulse control allows persons to react according to reason, not just emotion, and particularly in consideration of probable consequences. Children acquire impulse control in stages, from birth through adulthood, through a learning process undergone at each new developmental stage. This "reacquisition" is necessary because, as children acquire capacities, their unfamiliarity with the consequences of newfound abilities results in inevitable "miscalculations," requiring parental or societal responses that define acceptable limits of behavior. During the years between twelve and fifteen, impulse control improves as adolescents struggle with new demands for self-direction and self-management. However, for some adolescents the process extends well into middle or late adolescence.

- Psychosocial Development. Adolescents generally are less mature in psychosocial development than adults are. This influences the way they approach decisions, particularly in the context of social relations. Several dimensions of psychosocial development are relevant in assessing youth culpability: risk perception and preference, future orientation, and response to adult and peer influence. Each of these factors may contribute to adolescent decisions that reflect immature judgment. Research evidence indicates that adolescents differ from adults in their perception of and attitude toward risk. Adolescents are less risk averse than adults in that they tend to weigh anticipated gains more heavily than losses in making choices when compared with adults. Youths also, on average, tend to be greater risk-takers, engaging more frequently in behaviors such as drunken driving and unprotected sex. Future orientation, the capacity and inclination to project events into the future and consider future consequences, increases in the period between childhood and young adulthood. Adolescents tend to focus on the short-term risks and benefits of decisions and to pay less attention to long-term consequences when compared with adults. Finally, adolescents differ from adults in the extent to which others, including adult authority figures and peers, influence their choices. Substantial evidence supports the conclusion that adolescents are more susceptible to influence from peers when compared with adults. This susceptibility increases in early adolescence as part of the process of individuating from parents; it peaks at about age fourteen and declines slowly thereafter.

Scott and Grisso also indicate that it is not possible to point to a particular age at which youths attain adult-like psychological capacities because the changes associated with the four spheres of development do not necessarily occur together, and even within spheres, different capacities may develop at different rates. In addition, there is a great deal of individual variability among youths at any given age in all spheres of development. Therefore, while lawmakers usually define immaturity through bright-line rules based upon age to establish the legal boundaries between childhood and adulthood, from a developmental perspective it is a convenient but imprecise marker of the maturation process.

THE ROLE OF YOUTHFUL OFFENDING IN ADOLESCENCE. Behavioral science research indicates that the process of identity formation in adolescence is an important factor in understanding youthful patterns of criminal conduct. This research points to the fact that criminal behavior is rare in childhood. Onset typically begins in early adolescence, increases through age sixteen, and declines sharply from age seventeen onward (for example, Jessor and Jessor 1977; Hirschi and Gottfredson 1983; Mulvey and La Rosa 1986; Moffitt 1993). In addition, self-report studies

(Moffitt 1993) indicate that most teenage males engage in some criminal conduct. Indeed, Moffitt refers to criminal behavior as "a normal part of teen life" (1993, 675). Moffitt explains that during adolescence, youth are striving for autonomy from parental and adult authority. During this period, they are inclined to mimic the conduct of their antisocial peers to break the ties of childhood and demonstrate that they can act independently. However, only a small subset of young offenders will persist in a life of crime. Based on these patterns, Moffitt offers a taxonomy of adolescent antisocial conduct that describes typical teenage lawbreakers as "adolescence-limited" offenders, while a much smaller group are "life-course-persistent" offenders. Most youths in the first group have little notable history of antisocial conduct in childhood, and, predictably, in late adolescence or early adulthood, they will "mature out" of their inclination to get involved in criminal activity. Moffitt's explanation supports the conclusion that much youth crime represents the experimentation in risky behavior that is a part of identity development but desists naturally as individuals develop a stable sense of self and maturity of judgment.

The Impact of Developmental Immaturity on Trial Competency

As discussed more fully in chapter 3, U.S. law requires that defendants must be competent to stand trial. While the Supreme Court has never addressed whether the adjudicative competency requirement applies to juvenile proceedings, it has become an important issue in juvenile proceedings as well as when youths are subject to transfer or waiver to an adult court for trial. In recent years, many state legislatures have established procedures that are more punitive for handling juvenile delinquents. Juvenile adjudications increasingly may be open to public access, be reported to schools or other agencies, become part of a sex offender registry, be considered in the preparation of future adult sentencing guideline reports, and become one strike relevant to "three-strikes and you're out" statutes. At the same time, many states have liberalized their transfer statutes so that the most serious or chronic juvenile offenders face trial in adult court.

In *Godinez v. Moran* (509 U.S. 389 [1993]), the Supreme Court's most recent decision concerning competence to stand trial, the court clarified the meaning: competence means not only understanding the nature of the proceedings and the ability to assist counsel but also the ability to grasp the implications of making important decisions that involve the waiver of constitutional rights such as the right to remain silent, pleading guilty in response to plea bargains, or forgoing counsel. Behavioral science research suggests that developmental immaturity affects competence to stand trial because young people's capacity for grasping the significance of decisions they must make has not yet matured.

THE MACARTHUR JUVENILE ADJUDICATIVE COMPETENCE STUDY. The most comprehensive study of age differences in competence to stand trial is the MacArthur Juvenile Adjudicative Competence Study conducted by the MacArthur Foundation Research Network on Adolescent Development and Juvenile Justice (2003). Researchers decided to examine empirically the theoretical relationship between developmental immaturity and the abilities of young defendants to participate in their trials (Grisso et al. 2003). The study included 927 youths and 466 adults (aged eighteen to twenty-four) in four communities. Half of the study participants were in jail or detained in juvenile detention centers at the time of the study, and half were individuals of similar age, gender, ethnicity, and social class but residing in the community. The youth participants included three age categories—eleven to thirteen (20 percent of the youth sample), fourteen to fifteen (37 percent of the youth sample), and sixteen to seventeen (43 percent of the youth sample). These individuals were administered a standardized battery of tests designed to assess their knowledge and abilities relevant for competence to stand trial, their legal decision making in several hypothetical situations, and measures of a number of other characteristics that could potentially influence these capacities, such as intelligence and prior experience in the justice system (Grisso et al. 2003). Among the findings of the study were the following:

- Juveniles aged eleven to thirteen were more than three times as likely as young adults (individuals aged eighteen to twenty-four) to be "seriously impaired" on the evaluation of competence-relevant abilities, and juveniles aged fourteen to fifteen were twice as likely as young adults to be "seriously impaired."

- Individuals aged fifteen and younger differed from young adults in their legal decision-making. For example, younger individuals were less likely to recognize the risks inherent in different choices and less likely to think about the long-term consequences of their choices (for example, choosing between confessing versus remaining silent when being questioned by the police).

- Competence-relevant capacities of sixteen- and seventeen-year-olds as a group did not differ significantly from those of young adults.

- Juveniles of below-average intelligence were more likely to be "significantly impaired" in abilities relevant for competence to stand trial than juveniles of average intelligence. Because greater proportion of youths in the juvenile justice system than in the community were of below-average intelligence, the risk for incompetence to stand trial is even greater among adolescents who are in the justice system than it is among adolescents in the community.

- Performance on the evaluation did not vary as a function of individuals' gender, ethnicity, socioeconomic background, prior experience in the legal system, or symptoms of mental health problems.

Based on the results of the study, the MacArthur Foundation Research Network recommended that states consider implementing policies and practices designed to ensure that courts protect young defendants' rights to a fair trial. This may mean requiring competency evaluations for juveniles below a certain age before we decide to transfer them to adult court (Grisso et al. 2003, 350–60).

The Compounding Effects of Mental Illness and Developmental Immaturity

Behavioral science research also indicates that mental illness in childhood and adolescence is significantly different from the mental illness of adulthood, is often harder to identify, and is diagnosed less reliably. Grisso notes that when we prosecute youth with mental disorders as adults

> Cases of psychosis, especially schizophrenia, are frequently the focus of competence questions for adult defendants, but they are less common for adolescents outside of psychiatric hospitals. Nevertheless, disorders of childhood may negatively influence cognitive and emotional functioning no less seriously. Moreover, when youths face trial in adult courts, mental health professionals who examine them often do not have the clinical training and experience as well as forensic practice to prepare them to diagnose disorders of children and adolescents. Thus, youth in adult courts who have mental disorders are at a greater risk when compared with adults of having disorders not clinically diagnosed or misdiagnosed, with potential consequences for the fairness of their trials if their disorders impair their ability to participate in them. (2000, 426)

Recently, developmental psychopathology has emerged as a conceptual approach to correct the deficiencies in the diagnosis of mental disorders in youth (Cicchetti and Cohen 1995;

FOCUS 6.5. THE CASE OF LIONEL TATE AND
COMPETENCY TO STAND TRIAL

In 1999, a jury found Lionel Tate guilty of first-degree
murder for the killing of his playmate, Tiffany Eunich. The
sentence was controversial because Tate was twelve years
old at the time of the crime and his victim was six years
old. When he was found guilty at the age of fourteen, Lionel Tate became the youngest defendant ever sentenced to
life in prison in modern U.S. history. At trial, the evidence
presented indicated that Eunich had suffered as many as
thirty-five injuries, including a fractured skull, brain con-
tusions, bruises, a rib fracture, injuries to her knees and
pancreas, and a partially detached liver.

In 2004, the Court of Appeals of Florida reversed
and remanded. The question the court considered was
whether, due to Tate's extremely young age and lack of
previous exposure to the judicial system, a competency
evaluation was constitutionally mandated. This competency evaluation would determine whether Tate had sufficient present ability to consult with his lawyer with a
reasonable degree of rational understanding and whether
he had a rational, as well as factual, understanding of the
proceedings against him. Given the complexity of the legal
proceedings and his age, immaturity, and his nine- or ten-
year-old mental age, the appellate court determined that
such a hearing was mandated. The court noted that even
if a child of Tate's age had the capacity to understand less
serious charges, or commonplace juvenile court proceedings, a court cannot determine absent a hearing whether
that child could meet the competency standards incident
to facing a first-degree murder charge. It noted that this
charge involves profound decisions including whether to

make disclosures, intelligently analyzing plea offers, and deciding whether to waive important rights (*Tate v. Florida*, 864 So. 2d 44 [Fla. Dist. Ct. App. 2003]).

At the age of sixteen, the state of Florida released Lionel Tate from prison after he accepted a plea bargain and was sentenced to the three years he had already served. Other conditions of his plea bargain included ten years' probation, a year of house arrest, 1,000 hours of community service, and mandatory counseling sessions.

Cicchetti and Rogosch 2002). Developmental psychopathology is not merely the study of psychopathology in childhood and adolescence. Rather, it examines how "psychopathology emerges and changes in a developmental context, structured and guided by what is known about normal biological, cognitive, emotional, and social development during childhood, adolescence, and adulthood" (Grisso 2004, 30). Developmental psychopathologists emphasize that we should consider behaviors symptoms of disorder only to the extent that they deviate from normative behaviors of one's developmental peers, and that they are maladaptive only within the context of one's developmental period. So the developmental psychopathology perspective shifts away from seeing psychological disturbance during adolescence as either the grown-up version of childhood disorder or the immature counterpart of adult pathology. Instead, it is "the study of clinical phenomena in the context of adolescence as a developmental period" (Steinberg 2005, 124).

One significant consequence of a developmental approach is the need for ongoing research that examines the consequences of mental disorders with regard to the developmental factors in youths' decision-making processes as well as their competence

FOCUS 6.6. NETWORK ON ADOLESCENT
DEVELOPMENT AND JUVENILE JUSTICE

The John D. and Catherine T. MacArthur Foundation, a private, independent grant-making institution, sponsors the Research Network on Adolescent Development and Juvenile Justice. The network's purpose is to expand the base of knowledge about the origins, development, and treatment of juvenile crime and delinquency. In addition, the network aims to communicate the results of their research to policy makers, practitioners, journalists, and other social scientists and legal scholars to improve decision making in the current system and to prepare for the next generation of reform in juvenile justice policy and practice. The network brings together a broad spectrum of scholars, policy experts, and practitioners in social science, psychology, and the law. Three themes form the focus of its research. First, how do adolescents differ from adults in their capacity to understand and assist in the judicial process? Second, what is the actual and perceived culpability of adolescents involved in illegal activity? Third, how can we assess an individual's risk for future offending, the likelihood of changing his or her behavior, or the odds that he or she will respond to treatment? For more information on the network, see http://www.mac-adoldev-juvjustice. org/index.html.

to stand trial. Grisso (2004) argues that juveniles in the justice system face a kind of double jeopardy, with the effects of mental disorder potentially compounding the effects of immaturity on a juvenile's decisions. He maintains that many mental disorders may delay normal development and, therefore, it is likely that mental disorders among youths may have an impact on their cognitive and emotional development. Youths with mental disorders, therefore, may begin with a lower baseline when compared with adults, and any mental disorders simply compound the risks of immature decision making. We need to conduct additional empirical research on the possible compounding effect of various mental disorders on legally relevant abilities.

Incarcerated Youth with Mental Disorders

Youths accused of crimes are typically placed in juvenile detention facilities to await trial. The youth's age and the nature of the offense are factors that determine whether juvenile court or criminal court will hear the case and whether the sentence received is to a juvenile or adult correctional facility. In all three correctional settings—juvenile detention facilities, juvenile correctional facilities, and adult prisons—youth with mental disorders, like their adult counterparts, face little or no mental health treatment. They also frequently face deplorable conditions of confinement.

Placement of Youth with Mental Disorders in Juvenile Justice Facilities

Policy makers as well as researchers have documented the high rates of mental disorder among youths held in secure confinement and the lack of mental health services in both the community and the juvenile justice system. In July 2004, the U.S. House of Representatives Government Reform Committee published a report, *Incarceration of Youth Who Are Waiting for Community Mental Health Services in the United States*. It documented the inappropriate incarceration of these youths and concluded that the misuse of detention centers as holding areas for mental health treatment "is unfair to youth, undermines their health, disrupts the function of detention centers, and is costly to society" (U.S. House of Representatives 2004, 2).

Incarceration of Youth Who are Waiting for Mental Health Services in the United States was the first national study of its kind. It presented the results of a survey conducted by the Government Reform Committee covering the period from January 1 to June 30, 2003. The study defined "juvenile detention" as the holding of youths aged twenty-one and under in secure correctional facilities in three situations: without charges, pre-adjudication, or immediately post-adjudication. The survey did not survey the juvenile or adult prison system, where youth convicted of crimes may go to serve their sentences. Of 698 juvenile detention facilities identified in the United States, 524 juvenile detention administrators in forty-nine states, representing three-quarters of all juvenile detention facilities, responded.

The Government Reform Committee found that the use of juvenile detention facilities to house youth waiting for community mental health services is widespread and a serious national problem. More specifically, the committee found:

- Two-thirds of juvenile detention facilities held youths who were waiting for community mental health treatment. These facilities were located in forty-seven states. The legal status of incarcerated youths who were waiting for services varied. Two hundred and sixty-one facilities held youths waiting for community mental health services prior to their adjudication; 229 held such youths after adjudication. Seventy-one facilities in thirty-three states reported holding youths with mental disorders without any charges against them.

- Juvenile detention facilities frequently held young children because of the absence of community mental health services. One juvenile detention facility reported holding a seven-year-old child, 117 juvenile detention facilities reported holding children ten years and younger, and a majority of detention facilities reported holding children under thirteen years of age.

- Over a six-month period, nearly 15,000 incarcerated youths waited for community mental health services. Each night, nearly 2,000 youths waited in detention for community mental health services, representing 8 percent of all youth held in juvenile detention.
- Two-thirds of juvenile detention facilities that held youths waiting for community mental health services reported that some of these youths have attempted suicide or attacked others. Yet one-quarter of these facilities provided no or poor-quality mental health services, and over half of the facilities reported inadequate levels of staff training.
- Juvenile detention facilities spend an estimated $100 million each year to house youths who are waiting for community mental health services. This estimate does not include any of the additional expense in service provision and staff time associated with holding youths in urgent need of mental health services.
- Administrators of juvenile detention facilities reported frustration with the incarceration of youths who are waiting for mental health services. These administrators reported that they cannot detain these youths in a hospital setting because of their behaviors, but, at the same time, it is unsafe for them and staff to remain at the detention center.

The report concluded with a statement of the urgent need for major improvements in community mental health services to prevent the unnecessary and inappropriate incarceration of children and youth (U.S House of Representatives 2004, 4–15).

The report of the Government Reform Committee echoed earlier research that has consistently found high rates of mental disorder among youths held in juvenile detention facilities. For example, Otto and colleagues' (1992) review of thirty-four studies suggested that the rates of mental disorders among youths in the juvenile justice system are two to three times higher than

among youths in the general population. Other research estimates that anywhere from 70 to 100 percent of the youths in the
juvenile justice system have a diagnosable mental health disorder
(Otto et al. 1992; Abram and Teplin 1991; Teplin et al. 2002;
Virginia Policy Design Team 1994) and at least one out of every
five youths in the juvenile justice system has a serious mental
disorder (Cocozza and Skowyra 2000). Many of the youths in
the juvenile justice system are also experiencing some co-occurring
substance abuse disorder (Milin et al. 1991). A 1999 survey of
parents of mentally ill youths by the National Alliance for the
Mentally Ill (NAMI) found that 36 percent of their respondents
reported placing their children in the juvenile justice system
in order to access mental health services that were otherwise
unavailable to them (NAMI 1999). This research and the report
of the Government Reform Committee suggest that the juvenile justice system is becoming the system of "last resort" for
many young people with mental disorders.

Conditions of Confinement for Mentally Ill Juveniles

Mentally ill youth placed in the juvenile justice system often
experience inadequate mental health treatment and deplorable
conditions of confinement. The U.S. Department of Justice has
investigated the conditions of confinement for juveniles pursuant to its authority under the Civil Rights of Institutionalized
Persons Act (CRIPA) enacted in 1980. Under CRIPA, the attorney general through its Civil Rights Division has authority to
investigate conditions in public residential facilities and to take
appropriate action if a pattern or practice of unlawful conditions
deprives persons confined in the facilities of their constitutional
or federal statutory rights. Institutions covered under CRIPA
include jails, prisons, and juvenile justice facilities.

Since the law's enactment, the Civil Rights Division has
investigated hundreds of complaints concerning the conditions of
confinement in juvenile justice facilities; typically investigations

begin after reports of deplorable conditions in facilities. These include investigations of the mistreatment of mentally ill youth such as placing naked youths in crisis units, shackling them to beds and toilets, and excessive use of bodily restraints and punishment for behaviors resulting from specific mental disorders. In its report for 2003, the division monitored compliance with CRIPA consent decrees, settlement agreements, and court orders designed to remedy unlawful conditions in thirty-one juvenile justice facilities. The division initiated new investigations in two juvenile justice facilities and issued findings letters setting forth the results of its investigations regarding eleven juvenile justice facilities. In these investigations, the division made significant findings of constitutional deficiencies. It found

> that staff hog-tied youth and shackled youth to poles in public places. Girls were punished for their suicidal behavior by being stripped and placed naked, for extended periods of time, in a windowless, empty cell, called the "dark room," with only a hole in the floor to use as a toilet. Girls were forced to eat their own vomit if they threw-up while exercising in the hot sun. Staff used excessive force with impunity. Upon re-commitment to the facilities, youth were taken to the intake area and punched and slapped by staff and punishment for re-commitment. Abusive staff members were not terminated because there was a severe staffing shortage. The dental clinic at one juvenile justice facility was full of mouse droppings, dead roaches, and cobwebs; medications in the cabinet had expired 10 years ago. (U.S. Department of Justice 2003, 13–14)

In one case, the division filed a complaint and is monitoring a settlement agreement in Arkansas concerning the Alexander Youth Services Center. The agreement requires, in part, that the state revise the juvenile suicide prevention policy and provide

FOCUS 6.7. INCARCERATED MENTALLY ILL YOUTH: CONSTITUTIONAL ISSUES

Consider the case of *A.M. v. Luzerne County Juvenile Detention Center* (372 F.3d 572 [3d Cir. 2004]), involving a mentally ill juvenile.

Police arrested the juvenile, A.M., in Luzerne County, Pennsylvania, for indecent assault and he was taken to a secure detention facility for children alleged to be delinquent. He remained at the facility for thirty-eight days. While there, other juvenile residents physically assaulted A.M..—then thirteen years old—on numerous occasions. A.M. had a history of psychiatric inpatient hospitalizations for behavior problems prior to his detention. He was also taking psychotropic medication. The detention center's administrators received information about his psychiatric history upon his admission to the center, but A.M. did not receive his prescribed medication or other mental health treatment.

A.M. filed a federal civil rights suit against the county juvenile detention center alleging that they violated his due process rights by failing by failing to protect him from harm while he was detained at the detention center. The district court dismissed the suit. A.M. appealed. The Third Circuit Court of Appeals reversed.

The Third Circuit held that the evidence—in particular, the numerous incident reports—supported A.M.'s contention that the child-care workers at the center failed to intervene when altercations between A.M. and other residents began. The court held that a county could be liable for deficient hiring and staffing policies and practices, lack of adequate training programs for the detention center's staff, lack of established protocols to ensure safety, and lack of established policies to address the mental and physical health needs of residents.

mental health treatment to all juveniles who require such care (U.S. Department of Justice 2003, 4). In Louisiana, the division filed a settlement agreement requiring the state to enhance its efforts to reduce violence, expand staff training, and improve medical and mental health services at four juvenile justice facilities located in Tallulah, Baton Rouge, Monroe, and Bridge City. The court appointed an independent monitor to assemble a team of juvenile justice experts to provide technical assistance to the state agency operating the facilities, as well as review the state's compliance with the terms of the settlement (4–5).

In 2004, the Civil Rights Division investigated conditions at three secure juvenile justice facilities in New Mexico. The division conducted on-site inspections of the facilities with expert consultants in juvenile justice, suicide prevention, education, mental health, and medical care and issued its findings and minimal remedial steps necessary to address the deficiencies it found. The division found that the three facilities were inadequate in the following areas: suicide prevention, juvenile justice constitutional protections (for example, failure to protect youth from being sexually abused and unsanitary living conditions), education, medical care, and mental health/rehabilitative services. At one of the facilities, the division found that three youths had committed suicide between April 2002 and March 2003 (two with a sheet and one by strangling himself with his own belt). The division found that there was inadequate monitoring by the mental health staff of the facility. Youths with histories of depression and self-harm were not placed on suicide prevention or monitored by mental health staff. Moreover, the on-site investigation found that even when professionals monitored youths, they failed to document their clinical assessments. In terms of mental health care of all youths in the three facilities, the division found that the mental health services provided were inadequate to address the individual needs at each of the three facilities. The division identified the shortfalls in the areas of rehabilitative services, including inadequate group and individual therapy, interventions, interdisciplinary communication, and discharge planning (U.S. Department of Justice 2004, 4–35).

Juvenile Suicide in Confinement

Suicide is a major problem for mentally ill youth in juvenile justice facilities. In 2004, the Office of Juvenile Justice and Delinquency Prevention published the results of a study on juvenile suicide in confinement conducted by the National Center on Institutions and Alternatives. The report, *Juvenile Suicide in Confinement: A National Survey*, was the first comprehensive effort to determine the scope and distribution of suicides by youths confined in public and private juvenile facilities. The primary purpose of the study was to determine the "extent and distribution of juvenile suicides in confinement . . . as well as to gather descriptive data on demographic characteristics of each victim, characteristics of the incident, and characteristics of the juvenile facility which sustained the suicide" (Office of Juvenile Justice and Delinquency Prevention 2004, ix). The study identified 110 juvenile suicides occurring between 1995 and 1999 and analyzed data on 79 of these cases. Among the findings of the study are the following:

- 69.6 percent of victims were confined on nonviolent offenses.
- Approximately two-thirds (67.1 percent) of all victims were held on commitment status at time of death, with 32.9 percent held on detained status.
- 78.5 percent of victims had a history of prior offenses; most (76.3 percent) were of a nonviolent nature.
- 87.9 percent of victims had a substance abuse history; 22.7 percent of victims had a medical history; 58.3 percent of victims had an emotional abuse history; 43.5 percent had a physical abuse history; and 38.6 percent had a sexual abuse history.

- 74.3 percent of victims had a history of mental illness (with most thought to be suffering from depression at the time of death); 53.5 percent of victims were taking psychotropic medication.
- 98.7 percent of suicides were by hanging; 71.8 percent of victims used their bedding as the instrument.
- None of the victims were under the influence of alcohol or drugs at the time of the suicide.
- 74.7 percent of victims were assigned to single-occupancy rooms.
- Although the vast majority (78.5 percent) of respondents reported that their facilities maintained a written suicide prevention policy at the time of the suicide, only 20.3 percent

---

FOCUS 6.8. MENTALLY ILL YOUTH IN ADULT PRISONS

On November 26, 2002, Alexander Williams, thirty-four, hanged himself in his prison cell at the Georgia State Prison in Reidsville, Georgia. Williams was serving a sentence for the rape and murder of a sixteen-year-old girl. Williams was seventeen years old and mentally ill at the time the crime was committed. Diagnosed as a paranoid schizophrenic, Williams experienced hallucinations and was hearing voices several months prior to the crime. The state of Georgia sentenced Williams to death, but his case drew national attention from death penalty opponents. He would have been the first person in the United States to be forcibly medicated to make him sane enough for execution. Just days before his scheduled execution, the state Board of Pardons and Paroles commuted his sentence to life in prison (American Bar Association, http://www.abanet.org/crimjust/juvjus/williams.html).

of facilities had all seven suicide prevention components (written policy, intake screening, training, CPR certification, observation, safe housing, and mortality review) in place at the time of the suicide. (ix–xi)

The study offered several recommendations including that all juvenile facilities have all seven suicide prevention components in their suicide prevention policy and that future efforts should be directed at determining the effect of prolonged room confinement on suicidal behavior (Office of Juvenile Justice and Delinquency Prevention 2004, 38–42).

CONCLUSION AND IMPLICATIONS

This chapter has considered the colliding perspectives of criminal law and the behavioral sciences in terms of how each discipline considers the criminal culpability or blameworthiness of juvenile offenders, especially mentally ill juvenile offenders. How criminal law has viewed the criminal culpability of juvenile offenders has changed over time. Use of a historical perspective reveals that law has shifted its interpretation of youths' culpability based on changing public and political sentiments. Most recently, law increasingly views young people, especially adolescents, as no different from adults in terms of their blameworthiness. An emphasis on individual accountability that assumes free will has replaced an earlier image of youthful offending as resulting from insufficient moral training. This view conflicts with the assumptions and research of the behavioral sciences. Grounded in the empirical world, behavioral science examines the blameworthiness of youths from the perspective of developmental psychology. It offers a very different view of youth culpability, one that considers the cognitive and emotional factors that guide youths' decision making.

Behavioral science research also warns that mentally ill youth may face a kind of double jeopardy, with the effects of mental illness compounding normal cognitive and emotional development. However, the effect of mental disorders on normal cognitive and emotional development is part of an ongoing investigation on youth blameworthiness. Unfortunately, one of the consequences of our current justice policy is that mentally ill youths, like their adult counterparts, receive little or no treatment while incarcerated, face deplorable conditions of confinement, and have a high rate of suicide while incarcerated.

CHAPTER 7

Criminalizing Mental Illness

DOES IT MATTER?

> I truly regret that this had to happen, . . .
> [e]verybody trying to do the right thing and
> going through all the right steps and coming
> out with the wrong result. I think a simple
> I'm sorry would never be enough.
>
> —District Attorney Frank J. Clark*

ON FEBRUARY 6, 1987, a jury found Anthony
Capozzi, a schizophrenic, guilty of raping two women in 1983
and 1984. The trial judge sentenced him to eleven to thirty-
five years in prison. On April 2, 2007, Judge Shirley Troutman
threw out the rape convictions after DNA evidence linked the
crimes to another man. Capozzi spent twenty years in Attica
Correctional Facility, a maximum-security prison, for crimes he
did not commit. During his incarceration, the New York State
Parole Board denied him parole five times since he became eli-
gible in 1997, because his refusal to admit the crimes made it
impossible to complete a mandatory sex offender program. A
story in the *New York Times* on March 29, 2007, reported that

---

*Erie County district attorney's after a court hearing in Buffalo, New
York in which Judge Shirley Troutman threw out Anthony Copozzi's
two 1987 rape convictions ("After 22 years in prison, man exoner-
ated," CNN.com, April 3, 2007)

Capozzi's lawyer, Thomas D'Agostino, said upon learning of the DNA evidence, "Anthony has never, ever wavered. . . . He has known what it would mean to say, 'I did it.' If he said that, he would have gotten out. And he wouldn't do it."

Originally suspected in six attacks that took place in or near Delaware Park in Buffalo in 1983 and 1984, he faced trial for three rapes but juries only convicted him of two. His family always maintained his innocence. They argued that his mental illness made him incapable of planning the attacks in which the rapist threatened victims with a gun, took them to a secluded area, and ordered them to remain on the ground for ten to twenty minutes after the rape. The victims identified Capozzi in two police lineups. At the time of his trial, Capozzi had a three-inch vertical scar above his left eye. The victims who testified did not mention the scar and estimated the weight of their attacker at 150 pounds, at least 50 pounds less than what Capozzi weighed at the time. Capozzi's lawyer stated that there was no physical evidence linking Capozzi to the rapes. But the identification by the victims was the basis for the convictions.

An arrest of a suspect for another series of rapes and murders led to Capozzi's exoneration. Police arrested Altemio Sanchez after DNA evidence identified him as a rapist and serial killer known as the Bike Path Rapist. After that arrest, investigators began to question Capozzi's conviction because of the similarity between the rapes. At the time of Capozzi's trial, science had not developed the kind of DNA analysis that could demonstrate conclusively that Capozzi did not commit the crimes. However, beginning in the mid-1990s, the district attorney issued several subpoenas to the Erie County Medical Center for slides that contained genetic material from the rapes because DNA analysis could now establish Capozzi's guilt or innocence. Each time, the hospital reported that it did not have the slides. After the arrest of Sanchez, the district attorney once again issued a subpoena to the hospital. This time a pathologist at the hospital found slides

---

FOCUS 7.1. PRESIDENT BUSH'S NEW FREEDOM
COMMISSION ON MENTAL HEALTH

Pursuant to executive order, President George W. Bush's
New Freedom Commission on Mental Health conducted
a comprehensive study to evaluate the United State's mental health care system. In announcing the formation of
the commission, the president noted that "mental illness is
treatable, especially when the treatment comes early" (2).
The commission's report characterized the current mental
health system as "fragmented and in disarray . . . leading to
unnecessary and costly disability, homelessness, school failure and incarceration" (11). The report, however, did not
consider mentally ill criminal offenders (President's New
Freedom Commission on Mental Health 2004, http://
mentalhealth.about.com/library/free/blFullReport.htm).

---

containing genetic material from hundreds of rapes between
1973 and 2002, including those rapes attributed to Capozzi.
DNA analysis of the slides matched Sanchez and not Capozzi.
Shortly after, the district attorney joined with Capozzi's defense
counsel in asking for Capozzi's exoneration and release from
prison. After his release, he returned to Buffalo to reunite with
his family.

SOCIAL CONTROL AND THE SOCIAL MEANING OF MENTAL ILLNESS

While the mentally ill are not the only persons wrongly
convicted of crimes, research indicates that they are more
vulnerable to such convictions (Radelet et al. 2001; Scheck,
Neufeld, and Dwyer 2001). Our belief that the mentally ill are
dangerous creates a presumption of guilt in our minds even

when the suspect does not exactly match the physical characteristics of the perpetrator. In addition (although this did not happen in the *Capozzi* case), mentally ill individuals are more likely to confess to crimes that they did not commit during police interrogation (Redlich 2004).

Cases like *Capozzi* are newsworthy for a time because they highlight a clear injustice. Public discourse focuses on the specific events surrounding the injustice, but the discourse does nothing to change the fact that, essentially, prisons function as our asylum system. We criminalize the mentally ill because we are living in an era that emphasizes personal responsibility, and explanations for criminal conduct related to mental illnesses are viewed with heavy skepticism. Prisons became asylums because we consider mental illness to reflect a failure of responsibility—a loss of control over the kind of self required for successful adaptation to our society's values and norms. The dominance of the punitive model of mental illness reflects a shift toward a more punitive policy for all criminal offenders. However, as we suggested at the onset of this book, competing societal values are a part of our legal consciousness and create strain when we recognize the problematic nature of our policies concerning the mentally ill. If we consider the case of Andrea Yates, for example, competing values clearly entered into the jury's decision in the second trial. These competing values acknowledge the importance social environment, individual psychology, and biology in assessing the criminal responsibility of the mentally ill. These values have a long tradition in our culture despite their problematic and controversial nature under the punitive model.

Perlin (2000), a legal critic of current mental disability law, claims that the dominance of the punitive model creates a mental disability policy that is incoherent and contradictory. While the punitive model dominates our thinking, questions persist that have implications for mentally ill defendants, their victims, and society. Thinking back to the cases used as introductions to each of the chapters of this book, we can ask the following questions: Why was there no follow-up on Seung-Hui Cho after his release from involuntary commitment to see if he was receiving outpatient treatment? Why did psychiatric facilities release Andrew Goldstein from treatment so many times even though he wanted to stay in the hospital? Why didn't the criminal justice system provide treatment for Ralph Tortorici while he was in jail for eleven months awaiting trial? Why didn't psychiatrists see the danger that Andrea Yates posed to her children? Is Leroy Hendricks mentally ill or just dangerous, and who should decide, law or the behavioral sciences? How did Kip Kinkel's psychiatric problems become so easily dismissed prior to the killings and during his trial?

These cases and the questions posed by their tragic outcomes dramatize the failure of our current policies and the continuing conflict between law and the behavioral sciences. The mentally ill criminal defendant in today's courtroom faces an unpredictable outcome because of a confused body of law on issues bearing on criminal responsibility. In the areas of competency and the insanity defense, for example, the evolution of the law described in chapters 3 and 4 presents a conflicted portrait of how we view the mentally ill defendant. We have changed the common law meaning of blameworthiness to a simplified view of *mens rea,* dismissing the fact that common law tied the guilty mind to such ideas as volition and emotion. Law is skeptical of science-based insights and, at the same time, displays confusion about their meaning. In 2007, for example, the Supreme Court decided two cases that involved the death penalty and, to some degree, questions about mental capacity. In *Panetti v. Quarterman* (127 S. Ct. 2842 [2007]), discussed in chapter 3, a 5-to-4 court had to decide the issue of whether competency requires a defendant to possess both a factual and rational understanding of the criminal process in order to be competent for execution. The court decided that the Constitution requires both. However,

Justice Kennedy, writing for the majority, attempted to foreclose any debate about which mental states may qualify as competence by stating, "The beginning of doubt about competence in a case like petitioner's is not misanthropic personality or amoral character. It is psychotic disorder" (*Panetti v. Quarterman,* 127 S. Ct. 2862). Nevertheless, the court's decision in *Schriro v. Landrigan* (127 S. Ct. 1933 [2007]), illustrates that the *Panetti* decision did not end the debate about mental states. In *Schriro,* a 5-to-4 Supreme Court decided whether Jeffrey Landrigan's attorney provided ineffective assistance of counsel by failing to investigate and provide mitigating evidence concerning Landrigan's purported antisocial personality disorder even though Landrigan instructed his attorney not to provide such evidence. In deciding the issue, the Supreme Court held that no violation of ineffective counsel had occurred and found that Landrigan had clearly waived his right to present mitigating evidence. In dissent, Justice Stevens wrote that Landrigan's purported antisocial personality disorder was a "serious organic brain syndrome" and should have been further investigated and presented by Landrigan's counsel. In no less than seven instances, the dissenting opinion referred to Landrigan's antisocial personality disorder as a "serious organic brain syndrome." A reasonable reading of the term suggests that the dissent was implying that Landrigan was unable to control his behavior because it was the product of a brain disease on a par with epilepsy. Indeed, the dissent points to a psychological report prepared for the defense claiming that Landrigan's violence likely stemmed from a genetic disposition.

Two issues regarding the relationship between law and the behavioral sciences emerge from the *Panetti* and *Schriro* decisions. The first concerns the confusion about mental states and mental illness. The court tries to set some boundaries around these ideas in *Panetti* while the dissent in *Schriro* wants to open up the possibilities. Some of the court's confusion stems from the presentation of the behavioral sciences. The number of mental *disorders* contained in the *Diagnostic and Statistical Manual for Mental Disorders* (*DSM*), now in its fourth edition, continues to grow. When it was first published in 1952, the *DSM* contained 106 mental disorders. It was also the first time the term mental disorder was used in place of terms like mental illness or mental disease. Since then, the number of diagnosable mental disorders has grown substantially, with the current edition containing 297 mental disorders. Courts, both judges and juries, are unable to differentiate these disorders when the issue bears on criminal responsibility, as the *Panetti* and *Schriro* decisions illustrate.

The second issue illustrated in the *Panetti* and *Schriro* decisions is perhaps the more important one: how courts use behavioral science to further their own ends by using terminology that suggest a legitimate scientific classification of behavior. In the *Schriro* dissent, Justice Stevens uses what he considers behavioral science research regarding antisocial personality disorder as his rationale. In other words, one consequence of the behavioral science expansion of mental disorders and its research on them is their use by the legal system to justify its moral reasoning. When the *DSM* abandoned the term mental disease in favor of mental disorder, perhaps few understood the consequences of that change. As psychological science has moved further away from the concept of disease in describing abnormal behavior toward the almost boundless construct of disorder, law has advanced the idea of the biological basis for some deviant behaviors to justify certain controversial policies. For example, our legal system has adopted indefinite civil commitment for sex offenders not because they have a disease as conventionally construed but because state legislatures and courts postulate that there is some unknown mental abnormality that causes offenders to engage in the worst behavior imaginable against children.

These two issues illustrate an area of conflict between law and the behavioral sciences that, in all probability, is irresolvable: the kinds of mental states and the labels or categories that

FOCUS 7.2. THE MENTALLY ILL OFFENDER
TREATMENT AND CRIME REDUCTION ACT OF 2004

Congress responded to the issue of the criminalization of
the mentally ill by passing the Mentally Ill Offender Treatment and Crime Reduction Act of 2004. The president
signed it into law on October 30, 2004. The act authorizes
a $50 million federal grant program for states and counties
to establish more mental health courts and expand prisoners' access to mental health treatment while incarcerated
and upon reentry into the community. It provides additional resources for pretrial jail diversion programs and
related initiatives, and funds cross-training for law enforcement officials and mental health personnel dealing with
adult and juvenile offenders with mental health disorders.
In late November 2006, Congress passed and President
Bush signed into law the Science, State, and Justice Appro-
priations Act, which included $5 million in funding for
the Mentally Ill Offender Treatment and Crime Reduction Act. This is the first appropriation that the program,
passed in 2004, has received. For further information, see
http://www.apa.org/monitor/feb06/treatment.html.

criminal law should use in making determinations. Moreover,
as behavioral scientists to continue their investigation regarding
the biological basis for behavior, the conflict between law and
the behavioral sciences in these areas is likely to intensify. Law
stands predominately for freedom of the will. Behavioral science
is essentially a positive science. Law and the behavioral sciences
remain in polarized worlds.

Pustilnik (2005), a critic of our current punitive policy
toward the mentally ill, suggests that until there is a shift in the

way that the general culture thinks about mental illness, a transition from the moral/punitive conception to a medical/therapeutic model will not occur. People with mental illnesses will remain shut up in actual prisons and they will remain trapped in our thoughts about them. To get the mentally ill out of prison, she says we need to "think them out first," which means first thinking our way out of the conventional attitude that intersects mental illness and punishment. We must change the social meaning of mental illness in our consciousness. Policymakers in both criminal law and mental health need to become involved in reshaping our thinking and policy.

Relying on the adversarial system to reshape policy reinforces differences between the systems of criminal law and the behavioral sciences concerning the criminal responsibility of mentally ill defendants. One way to understand the *Panetti* and *Schriro* decisions is to realize that law holds the trump card when the issue is how to consider the mental state of a person after the crime is committed. Once a mentally ill person commits a crime, the criminal justice system takes over, and the role of the behavioral sciences becomes embedded in an adversarial system. Behavioral science experts must try to convey their point of view from within the confines of our system of criminal law. For example, social context is lost in determining guilt or innocence. It does not matter, for the most part, whether the defendant's background is poor, minority, or in other ways marginalized. Law only asks about *mens rea, actus reus,* and the evidence to determine the defendant's guilt and the appropriate punishment.

Alternatively, behavioral sciences can help prevent the issue from reaching the courts by providing the policy initiatives and rationales that convince state legislators to enact laws that will prevent criminal acts by the mentally ill. The behavioral sciences understand and appreciate the social context for mental illness and criminal behavior. They also know about the limitations of current involuntary civil commitment laws, the weaknesses of assisted outpatient treatment laws, and the poor quality of mental health care in many communities. Even once criminal acts are committed, it is the behavioral sciences that can tell us, although imperfectly, what can work in the treatment and/ or rehabilitation of mentally ill offenders. On one issue it is safe to say we share consensus: we want to prevent future crimes by the mentally ill. Focusing on prevention is a method of changing our legal consciousness from a punitive model of mental illness to a therapeutic one.

THERAPEUTIC JURISPRUDENCE: MENTAL HEALTH COURTS

One recent policy initiative that focuses on prevention is the creation of jail diversion programs, most notably the creation of mental health courts. In 2000, Congress authorized the attorney general to make grants available for up to one hundred mental health courts in the National Law Enforcement and Mental Health Act (Pub. L. No. 106–515 [2000]). Congress passed the act because a number of groups had voiced their concern over the growing number of mentally ill confined in jails and prisons where proper psychiatric care was minimal or nonexistent. The goals of mental health courts are twofold. First, they aim to break the cycle of worsening mental illness and criminal behavior that begins with the failure of community mental health systems and accelerates with the inadequacy of treatment in jails and prisons. Second, mental health courts are to provide effective treatment options instead of the usual criminal sanctions for mentally ill offenders. In 2005, there were 113 mental health courts in the United States (National GAINS Center 2006).

In order to accomplish these goals, the act called for continuing judicial supervision of qualified nonviolent offenders with mental disabilities. It also called for the creation of coordinated programs to train court and law enforcement personnel to recognize offenders with mental health needs, to provide voluntary mental health treatment as a "meaningful diversion" from criminal sanctions, to centralize case management processes, and to provide continuity in psychiatric care following release (Slate 2003).

Structure and Operation of Mental Health Courts

There are some general principles that most mental health courts possess which make them different from traditional trial courts. One of the primary differences is a deemphasis on the adversarial approach typical in criminal cases. Mental health courts discourage aggressive defense counsel actions, such as suppression motions, in favor of a collaborative approach in which defense counsel's primary role is to advocate for the defendant's wishes regarding treatment. In addition, defense counsel often help persuade their clients to participate in treatment. Thus, counsel may request the court to consider a client for supervised housing, urine toxicology screens for illicit drugs, or outpatient commitment in addition to primary psychiatric care (Slate 2003, 16–18).

Before a typical mental health session, a variety of representatives from various mental health agencies gather in chambers to review with the supervising judge the appropriateness of new program participants, the progress of current participants, and strategies to deal with participants who are noncompliant with treatment or who cannot be located. The prosecutor and defense counsel are also present but in a reduced capacity. Defense counsel may request changes or additions to a client's treatment, but there is no formal means for petitioning these changes or additions from the court. Likewise, the prosecutor may voice opposition to a particular treatment approach but has little recourse in altering the court's discretion. Thus, mental health courts vastly reduce the typical role of both prosecutor and defense counsel.

Usually, defendants in mental health courts have routine "status" hearings in which representatives report to the judge the level of participation in treatment of the defendant. Many of these hearings are dedicated to ascertaining whether a defendant is compliant with their prescribed medication and has failed any recent (usually routine) screens for illicit drugs. These status hearings occur at the discretion of the judge and can be as frequent as biweekly or as infrequent as biannually. During status hearings, the court generally does not follow formal rules of evidence. The intent is to permit the judge to have all relevant information so that he or she can make treatment decisions. For example, these courts permit hearsay evidence to inform the court as to the progress of a defendant in treatment, his or her history related to treatment issues, and suspected illicit drug use or other criminal activity (Slate 2003, 17).

Treatment in mental health courts often relies upon forms of outpatient care that provide for close supervision of the mentally ill and that usually have intensive treatment programs already in place in the community. Another option at the court's disposal is the use of assertive programs that emphasize bringing mental health treatment to the patient, relying upon mobile treatment teams in the community. An additional option is the use of mental health case managers to connect clients to residential, financial, and other needed services in the community. With treatment at the forefront, the prospect of trial fades. The majority of the courts' resources are directed at obtaining services that are likely to help the defendant manage his or her mental illness.

Since mental health courts are a relatively new development, little empirical evidence exists regarding their effectiveness. Research seems to indicate that these courts may be effective in diverting individuals from jails and prisons. However, little evidence exists concerning whether psychiatric symptoms improve for the individuals who participate in these courts (Moore and

Hiday 2006; Redlich et al. 2006; Boothroyd, Mercado et al. 2005; Christy et al. 2005; Steadman, Redlich et al. 2005; Boothroyd, Poythress et al. 2003; Griffin, Steadman, and Petrila 2002).

Constitutional Concerns

Many jurisdictions only allow a potential candidate to enter a mental health court if they agree to plea bargain to a lesser charge. Often the plea is very generous, allowing a defendant to plea to a charge that may carry a potential maximum penalty of a small monetary fine. In some jurisdictions, including those that offer plea bargains, the court retains the right to reinstate the original charges if the defendant fails to engage in treatment. While such a measure is inconsistent with conventional rules of justice, many courts see this element as an essential piece of leverage to keep defendants in treatment. In addition, there are great differences among mental health courts as to how long monitoring by the court can occur. In many mental health courts, the court decides the length of monitoring on a case-by-case basis. While many mental health courts deal exclusively with defendants charged with violation or misdemeanor offenses, court monitoring generally lasts in excess of what a defendant would serve if convicted of the original charge (Erickson, Campbell, and Lamberti 2006, 338).

A frequent criticism of mental health courts is whether these courts are truly "voluntary" or whether they contain elements of coercion. Mental health courts rest on the assumption that the defendant's transfer to the court is voluntary. Otherwise, singling out defendants with mental illnesses for separate and different treatment would violate their constitutional rights and other legal rights. Yet truly voluntary transfers to mental health courts require more than simply a verbal declaration by defendants. Transfer contains risks, and defendants need to make informed decisions that require the ability to reason and assess consequences of decisions. While mentally ill defendants may appear to meet the legal standard for competency, their mental illness may nonetheless compromise cognitive and emotional abilities, especially the ability to reason clearly. Coercion may also be present in mental health courts when courts use their authority to compel treatment adherence. Mental health courts are in a precarious position in that they must balance the nontraditional role of acting as a therapeutic agent on the one hand and deliver sanctions for treatment noncompliance on the other. Moreover, there is concern about whether defendants can withdraw from participation in the mental health court and have their cases heard in criminal court without prejudice. In one study of mental health courts, 56 percent of the responding courts do not allow a defendant to reverse his or her decision and withdraw from the mental health court program without prejudice. Of the courts that permit withdrawal, many impose a time limitation for the decision or specify that withdrawal can only occur when participation is not a condition of probation (Erickson, Campbell, and Lamberti 2006, 340–42).

Given these important concerns, mental health courts are representative of current attempts to ease the punitive approach to the mentally ill by the criminal justice system. The aims of these interventions are well-intentioned and noble, but they inadvertently may undermine crucial Constitutional protections that safeguard defendants from improper prosecutions. The nexus of this contradiction lies in the need for these interventions to use legal leverage to encourage treatment adherence. Legal leverage ultimately means using the power of law to exact desired ends. Irrespective of whether those ends are therapeutic, noble, or well-intentioned, our constitutional criminal justice system recognizes the potential harm in the power of law lies as much (if not more) with *how* it achieves its end and not merely with what end is desired.

FOCUS 7.3. HURRICANE KATRINA, NEW ORLEANS, AND THE CRISIS IN MENTAL HEALTH CARE

On the two-year anniversary of Hurricane Katrina, National Public Radio reported on August 29, 2007, that mental health services are in short supply in New Orleans. Alix Spiegel described on the All Things Considered program that before the storm, there were 240 hospital psychiatric beds in Orleans Parish, but now there are only 30. With so few hospital beds for the mentally ill, some family members plot ways to get their family members put in jail, because the parish prison has 60 adult psychiatric beds where patients can get consistent care.

THE LIMITATIONS OF A THERAPEUTIC CULTURE

Mental health courts represent an example of policy initiatives that attempt to divert the mentally ill from jails and prisons by focusing on treatment and/or rehabilitation for the individual. The social construction of mental illness remains an "individuated-legal" construction and seeks to prevent criminalization of the mentally ill through programs designed to treat the person's "mental illness." Such an approach is consistent with how we currently frame social problems in our society. Rather than seeing them as embedded in structural inequality, we view social ills as rooted in individual pathology and rely on solutions like mental health courts to address the individuals who come to their attention. Sociologists and historians ascribe this shift in values and attitudes to a number of historical and social forces, among them the breakdown of social and community institutions that traditionally addressed problems like addiction, domestic violence, and mental illness.

As we have discussed throughout this book, our present-day emphasis on individual responsibility or "accountability" has its counterpart in how we view deviant behavior. In criminal justice, theories of criminal behavior that based deviance in personality or individualistic factors gained prominence over earlier accounts that depicted, for example, the harsh realities of inner-city life and its relationship to criminal behavior. Instead, explanations for criminal behavior focused on such psychological factors as the "bonds of the individual to society" (Hirschi 1969) or the ability of individuals to control "impulsive behavior" (Gottfredson and Hirschi 1990). In several legal settings, explanations of criminal behavior in individualistic terms create a disposition to see the "solution" or "cure" in terms of various psychological treatment modalities. In family court, for example, the laws concerning child abuse and child neglect encourage parents who abused or neglected their children to rehabilitate themselves through various treatment programs such as parenting classes, substance abuse programs, and domestic violence counseling. Although these parents typically live in poverty and have few if any support systems within their extended families or community, those absence of resources are not the focus of attention. Rather, courts assume that individualistic counseling and treatment programs can provide the solution to motivated and cooperating parents.

Shifting our legal consciousness of the mentally ill requires that we look to the tradition of sociological and criminological theory that understands the social context of mental illness. There is, first, a long tradition of social science research that examines the negative relationship of socioeconomic status (SES) with mental illness. The lower the SES of an individual, the higher is his or her risk of mental illness. Landmark studies conducted by Faris and Dunham (1939) in Chicago, Hollingshead and Redlich in New Haven, Connecticut (1958), and the Midtown Manhattan study (Srole et al. 1977) found dramatic differences in prevalence of mental illness between the lowest and highest social classes. More recently, this research has focused on clarifying the causal structure of the relationship (for example, Hudson 2005; Ritsher et al. 2001; Link, Lennon, and Dohrenwend 1993; Dembling et al. 2002). Do poor socioeconomic conditions predispose individuals toward mental illness? Alternatively, do preexisting, biologically based mental illnesses result in the drift of individuals into poor socioeconomic circumstances? While the conclusions from this research remain mixed, most studies have found evidence for the role of social causation in mental illness. Studies support the role of social selection for the major mental illnesses such as schizophrenia (Dohrenwend et al. 1992). Regardless of causation, this research clearly indicates the need for preventative and early intervention strategies of the major mental illnesses, especially strategies that pay attention to such factors as unemployment and housing, including homelessness.

In addition to understanding the relationship between social class and mental illness, there is also a need to apply criminological theory to assist in developing policy to focus on prevention. Fisher, Silver, and Wolff (2006) examine how we can apply criminological theory in order to move beyond criminalization of the mentally ill. Recognizing the relationship between social class and mental illness, they explore at a theoretical level the implications of this relationship using criminological theory. The note, for example, that the mentally ill often have access to subsidized housing in low-income areas. These residential programs may cluster in areas occupied by other low-income individuals. Importantly, individuals with severe mental illnesses residing in such neighborhoods are likely to be unemployed and may share their time with persons who may not have serious mental illnesses but who are subject to the same environmental risk factors. These may include social networks in which people use illicit drugs but lack the economic means to acquire them and thus engage in unlawful conduct, such as larceny and prostitution. The poor mentally ill may encounter other socially marginalized individuals who may introduce or model substance abuse and other criminal activities. Moreover, unemployed mentally individuals residing in low-income neighborhoods are likely to encounter others with unstructured time. Like the mentally ill, these individuals also may not have other levels of informal social control such as family. In other words, criminological theory informs us that both social capital and social networks may be the key determinants of the likelihood of criminal offending among the mentally ill (Fisher, Silver, and Wolff 2006, 12–14).

Diversion programs, therefore, need to address the social environments in which the mentally ill reside and interact. Such an approach requires an embrace of social-science-based insights in our public discourse about what to do about the problem of the seriously mentally ill in our society. These insights can assist us in understanding our tendency to place the mentally ill in either asylums or prisons and the problems that either policy creates. Focusing on prevention by addressing the social environments of the mentally ill also enables us to understand that we can prevent the kinds of criminal acts that we have described the case histories presented in this book. Finally, framing the issue of prevention in social science terms can take the debate out of the conflict between law and the behavioral sciences and into the formulation of policies that benefit not only the mentally ill but also our society.

In sum, our current policy of criminalization of the mentally ill is misguided because we do not have a criminologically informed approach to mental health policy and services that would recognize that the mentally ill are not identical to other citizens and thus require special treatment. Indeed, many of the older commitment laws were predicated on recognizing this difference, while much of the 1960s and 1970s "liberation" from psychiatry was guided by seeing the mentally ill as "the same" as everyone else. We used to treat the mentally ill with compassion because they were sick. The state served as their guardian because it recognized that they had a disability. All that changed when we "liberated" the mentally ill and treated them the same as everyone else. Now we use police powers to incapacitate the mentally ill, and we frame the problem of the mentally ill in terms of their risk for violence. As we widened the punitive net to include the mentally ill, we discounted the humanity of this class of social deviants. Does it matter that we criminalize the mentally ill? Yes, for several reasons described in this book. Above all, it is a statement about our social morality: the social meaning we construct and the social rules we use for the class of deviants we call the mentally ill.

References

Books and Journal Articles

Abram, K., and L. Teplin. 1991. Co-occurring disorders among mentally ill detainees. *American Psychologist* 46 (10): 1036–45.

Allen, M., and V. E. Smith. 2001. Opening Pandora's box: The practical and legal dangers of involuntary outpatient commitment. *Psychiatric Services* 52 (3): 342–46.

Amador, X. F., M. Flaum, N. C. Andreasen, D. H. Strauss, et al. 1994. Awareness of illness in schizophrenia and schizoaffective and mood disorders. *Archives of General Psychiatry* 51 (10): 826–36.

American Bar Association House of Delegates. 1983. *American Bar Association Policy on the Insanity Defense*. Chicago: American Bar Association.

American Law Institute. 1962. *Model Penal Code §4.01, Proposed Official Draft*. Philadelphia: American Law Institute.

American Medical Association. 1984. Committee on Medicolegal Problems. Insanity defense in criminal trials and limitations of psychiatric testimony: Report of Board of Trustees. *Journal of the American Medical Association* 251 (22): 2967–81.

American Medical Association. 1998. Council on Ethical and Judicial Affairs. E-2.06 Capital punishment. *American Medical Association Code of Ethics*. Chicago: American Medical Association.

American Psychiatric Association. 1968. *Diagnostic and Statistical Manual of Mental Disorders*. Washington, D.C.: American Psychiatric Association.

———. 1982. *Statement on the Insanity Defense*. Washington, D.C.: American Psychiatric Association.

———. 1983. American Psychiatric Association statement on the insanity defense. *American Journal of Psychiatry* 140 (6): 681–88.

———. 2000. *Psychiatric Services in Jails and Prisons*. Washington, D.C.: American Psychiatric Association.

———. 2004. *Diagnostic and Statistical Manual of Mental Disorders: DSM IV-Tr*. Washington, D.C.: American Psychiatric Association.

Applebaum, P. S., and T. G. Gutheil. 2006. *Clinical Handbook of Psychiatry and the Law*. New York: Lippincott, Williams, and Wilkins.

Bachrach, L. L. 1984. Asylum and chronically ill psychiatric patients. *American Journal of Psychiatry* 141 (8): 975–78.

Bassuk, E., and S. Gerson. 1978. Deinstitutionalization and mental health services. *Scientific American* 238: 46–53.

Bazelon, D. L. 1983. The dilemma of criminal responsibility. *Kentucky Law Journal* 77: 263–77.

Beccaria, C. 1963. *On Crimes and Punishments.* Trans. H. Paolucci. Englewood Cliffs, N.J.: Prentice-Hall.

Beck, A. J., and L. M. Maruschak. 2001. *Mental Health Treatment in State Prisons, 2000.* Washington, D.C.: U. S. Department of Justice, Bureau of Justice Statistics.

Becker, H. S. 1963. *Outsiders.* Studies in the sociology of deviance. New York: Free Press.

Bennett, W., J. J. DiIulio Jr., and J. P. Walters. 1996. *Body Count: Moral Poverty . . . and How to Win America's War against Crime and Drugs.* New York: Simon and Schuster.

Berger, P., and T. Luckmann. 1966. *The Social Construction of Reality.* Garden City, N.Y.: Doubleday.

Blackstone, W. 1769/1979. *Commentaries on the Laws of England, in Four Books,* vol. 4, *Of Public Wrongs.* Chicago: University of Chicago Press.

Boland, F. 1999. *Anglo-American Insanity Defence Reform: The War between Law and Medicine.* Brookfield, Vt.: Ashgate/Dartmouth.

Bonnie, R. J. 1992. The competence of criminal defendants: A theoretical reformulation. *Behavioral Sciences and the Law* 10 (3): 291–316.

Bonnie, R. J., and T. Grisso. 2000. Adjudicative competency and youthful offenders. In *Youth on Trial: A Developmental Perspective on Juvenile Justice,* edited by T. Grisso and R. G. Schwartz. Chicago: University of Chicago Press.

Bonnie, R., J. Jeffries, and P. Low. 2000. *The Trial of John W. Hinckley: A Case Study in the Insanity Defense.* New York: Foundation Press.

Boothroyd, R. A., C. C. Mercado, C. Calkins, N. G. Poythress, A. Christy, and J. Petrila. 2005. Clinical outcomes of defendants in mental health courts. *Psychiatric Services* 56 (7): 829–34.

Boothroyd, R. A., N. G. Poythress, A. McGaha, and J. Petrila. 2003. The Broward Mental Health Court: Process, outcomes, and service utilization. *Journal of Law and Psychiatry* 26 (1): 55–71.

Borum, R., M. Swartz, S. Riley, J. Swanson, V. A. Hiday, and R. Wagner. 1999. Consumer perceptions of involuntary outpatient commitment. *Psychiatric Services* 50 (11): 1489–91.

Bowman, K. M., and M. Rose. 1952. A criticism of current usage of the term "sexual psychopath." *American Journal of Psychiatry* 109 (3): 177–82.

Brakel, S. J. 2003. Competence to stand trial: Rationalism, "contextualism," and other modest theories. *Behavioral Sciences and the Law* 21 (3): 285–95.

Burdon, W. M., and C. A. Gallagher. 2002. Coercion and sex offenders: Controlling sex-offending behavior through incapacitation and treatment. *Criminal Justice and Behavior* 29 (1): 87–109.

Burns, K., and A. Bechara. 2007. Decision making and free will: A neuroscience perspective. *Behavioral Sciences and the Law* 25 (2): 263–80.

Caspi, A., J. McClay, T. E. Moffitt, J. Mill, J. Martin, I. W. Craig, A. Taylor, and R. Poulton 2002. Role of genotype in the cycle of violence in maltreated children. *Science* 297 (2): 851–54.

Cassel, E. 2003. Medicating the mentally ill for trial and execution: What are the implications of the Supreme Court's recent decision. Find Law: Legal News and Commentary, http://writ.news.findlaw.com/cassel/20030703.html.

Center for Sex Offender Management. 2006. *Understanding Treatment for Adults and Juveniles Who Have Committed Sex Offenses.* Washington, D.C.: U.S. Department of Justice.

Christy, A., N. G. Poythress, R. A. Boothroyd, J. Petrila, and S. Mehra. 2005. Evaluating the efficiency and community safety goals of the Broward County Mental Health Court. *Behavioral Sciences and the Law* 23 (2): 222–43.

Cicchetti, D., and D. J. Cohen. 1995. *Developmental Psychopathology.* New York: Wiley.

Cicchetti, D., and F. Rogosch. 2002. A developmental psychopathology perspective on adolescence. *Journal of Consulting and Clinical Psychology* 70 (1): 6–20.

Cirincione, C., H. J. Steadman, and M. A. McGreevy. 1995. Rates of insanity acquittals and the factors associated with successful insanity pleas. *Bulletin of American Academy of Psychiatry and Law* 23 (3): 399–409.

Cocozza, J. J., and K. R. Skowyra. 2000. Youth with mental health disorders: Issues and emerging responses. *Juvenile Justice* 7 (1): 3–13.

Cold killer's 20-mile trail leaves five dead. 2000. *Pittsburgh Post Gazette,* April 29.

Correctional Association of New York. 2004. *Mental Health in the House of Corrections: A Study of Mental Health Care in the New York State Prisons.* New York: Correctional Association of New York.

Cruise, K. R., and R. Rogers. 1998. An analysis of competence to stand trial: An integration of case law and clinical knowledge. *Behavioral Sciences and the Law* 16: 35–50.

D'Angelo, E. 1968. *The Problem of Freedom and Determinism.* Columbia: University of Missouri Press.

Dembling, B. P., V. Rovnyak, S. Mackey, and M. Blank. 2002. Effects of geographic migration on SMI prevalence estimates. *Mental Health Services Research* 4: 7–12.

Deutch, A. 1949. *The Mentally Ill in America: A History of Their Care and Treatment.* New York: Columbia University Press.

Ditton, P. M. 1999. *Mental Health and the Treatment of Inmates and Proba-tioners.* Washington, D.C.: U.S. Department of Justice, Bureau of Justice Statistics.

Dohrenwend, B. P., I. Levav, P. E. Shrout, S. Schwartz, G. Naveh, and B. G. Link. 1992. Socioeconomic status and psychiatric disorders: The causation-selection issue. *Science* 255: 946–52.

Dorf, M., and J. Fagan. 2003. Problem-solving courts: From innovation to institutionalization. *American Criminal Law Review* 40: 1501–11.

Draine, J. 1997. Conceptualizing services research on outpatient commitment. *Journal of Mental Health Administration* 24 (3): 306–15.

Engel, D. 1998. How does law matter in the constitution of legal consciousness. In *How Does Law Matter?* edited by B. G. Garth and Austin Sarat, 109–44, Evanston, Ill.: Northwestern University Press.

Erickson, P. E. 2001. The legal standard of volitional impairment: An analysis of substantive due process and the United States Supreme Court's decision in *Kansas v. Hendricks. Journal of Criminal Justice* 30: 1–10.

Erickson, S. K., A. Campbell, and J. S. Lamberti. 2006. Variations in mental health courts: Challenges, opportunities, and a call for caution. *Community Mental Health Journal* 42 (4): 335–44.

Ewing, C. P., and J. T. McCann. 2006. *Minds on Trial: Great Cases in Law and Psychology.* New York: Oxford University Press.

Fagan, J., and F. E. Zimring. 2000. *The Changing Borders of Juvenile Justice: Transfer of Adolescents to the Criminal Court.* Chicago: University of Chicago Press.

Faris, R.E.L., and W. W. Dunham. 1939. *Mental Disorders in Urban Areas.* Chicago: University of Chicago Press.

Ferro, J. 2005. *Sexual Misconduct and the Clergy.* New York: Facts on File.

Fingarette, H. 1972. *The Meaning of Criminal Insanity.* Berkeley: University of California Press.

Finkel, N. J. 1988. *Insanity on Trial.* New York: Plenum Press.

Fischer, P., and W. Breakey. 1986. Homelessness and mental health: An overview. *International Journal of Mental Health* 14 (4): 6–14.

Fisher, W. H., E. Silver, and N. Wolff. 2006. Beyond criminalization: Toward a criminologically informed framework for mental health policy and service research. *Administrative Policy Mental Health and Mental Health Services Research* 33: 544–47.

Foucault, M. 1965/1988. *Madness and Civilization: A History of Insanity in the Age of Reason.* New York: Vintage Books.

Fox, A., and M. W. Zawitz. 2002. *Homicide Trends on the United States: 2002 Update.* Washington, D.C.: U.S. Department of Justice, Bureau of Justice Statistics.

Furlong, F. W. 1981. Determinism and free will: Review of the literature. *American Journal of Psychiatry* 138: 435–39.

Goffman, E. 1961/1990. *Asylums: Essays on the Social Situation of Mental Patients and Other Inmates.* New York: Doubleday.

Golding, S. L. 1992. Studies of incompetent defendants: Research and social policy implications. *Forensic Reports* 21: 77–83.

Goldman, H. H. 1983. The multiple functions of the state mental hospital. *American Journal of Psychiatry* 140: 296–300.

Goldman, H. H., N. H. Adams, and C. A. Taube. 1983. Deinstitutionalization: The data demythologized. *Hospital and Community Psychiatry* 34 (2): 129–34.

Goldstein, A. S. 1967. *The Insanity Defense.* New Haven, Conn.: Yale University Press.

Goode, E. 1994. Moral panics: Culture, politics, and social construction. *Annual Review of Sociology* 20: 149–71.

Gottfredson, M., and T. Hirschi. 1990. *A General Theory of Crime.* Stanford, Calif.: Stanford University Press.

Grabosky, P. N. 1980. Rates of imprisonment and psychiatric hospitalization in the United States. *Social Indicators Research* 7: 63–70.

Green, T. A. 1995. Freedom and responsibility in the Age of Pound: An essay on criminal justice. *Michigan Law Review* 93: 1915–2033.

Griffin, P. A., H. J. Steadman, and J. Petrila. 2002. The use of criminal charges and sanctions in mental health courts. *Psychiatric Services* 53 (10): 1285–89.

Grisso, T. 2000. The changing face of juvenile justice. *Psychiatric Services* 51 (4): 425–38.

————. 2003. *Evaluating Competencies: Forensic Assessments and Instruments.* New York: Springer.

————. 2004. *Double Jeopardy: Adolescent Offenders with Mental Disorders.* Chicago: University of Chicago Press.

Grisso, T., L. Steinberg, J. Woolard, E. Cauffman, E. Scott, S. Graham, F. Lexce, N. D. Reppucci, and R. Schwartz. 2003. Juveniles' competence to stand trial: A comparison of adolescents' and adults' capacities as trial defendants. *Law and Human Behavior* 27 (4): 333–63.

Grisso, T., and R. G. Schwartz, eds. 2000. *Youth on Trial: A Developmental Perspective on Juvenile Justice.* Chicago: University of Chicago Press.

Grob, G. N. 1994. *The Mad among Us: A History of the Care of America's Mentally Ill.* New York: Free Press.

Gronfein, W. 1985. Psychotropic drugs and the origins of deinstitutionalization. *Social Problems* 32 (5): 437–54.

Grubin, D., and L. Madsen. 2006. Accuracy and utility of post-conviction polygraph testing of sex offenders. *British Journal of Psychiatry* 188: 479–83.

Guy, E., J. J. Platt, I. Zwerling, and S. Bullock. 1985. Mental health status of prisoners in an urban jail. *Criminal Justice and Behavior* 12: 29–53.

Hacking, I. 1999. *The Social Construction of What?* Cambridge, Mass.: Harvard University Press.

Hale, M. 1736/2003. *Historia Pacitorum Coronae: The History of the Pleas of the Crown*, vol. 1. Clark, N.J.: Lawbook Exchange.

Hans, V. P., and D. Slater. 1983. John Hinckley Jr. and the insanity defense: The public's verdict. *Public Opinion Quarterly* 47 (2): 202–12.

Hanson, R., and K. E. Morton-Bourgon. 2005. The characteristics of persistent sexual offenders: A meta-analysis of recidivism studies. *Journal of Consulting and Clinical Psychology* 73 (6): 1154–63.

Harcourt, B. E. 2006. From the asylum to the prison: Rethinking the incarceration revolution. *Texas Law Review* 84: 1751–85.

Hart, T. C., and C. Rennison. 2002. *Reporting Crime to the Police, 1922–2000.* Washington, D.C.: U.S. Department of Justice, Bureau of Justice Statistics.

Hiday, V. S. 1999. Mental illness and the criminal justice system. In A. V. Horowitz and T. L. Scheid, eds., *A Handbook for the Study of Mental Health: Social Contexts, Theories, and Systems.* New York: Cambridge University Press.

Hiday, V. S., and T. Scheid-Cook. 1987. The North Carolina experience with outpatient commitment: A critical appraisal. *International Journal of Law and Psychiatry* 10: 215–32.

Hirschi, T. 1969. *Causes of Delinquency.* Berkeley: University of California Press.

Hirschi, T., and M. Gottfredson. 1983. Age and the explanation of crime. *American Journal of Sociology* 89 (3): 552–70.

Hoge, M. A., and E. Grottole. 2000. The case against outpatient treatment. *Journal of the Academy of Psychiatry and the Law* 28 (2): 165–70.

Hollingshead, A. B., and F. C. Redlich. 1958. *Social Class and Mental Illness.* New York: Wiley.

Hudson, C. G. 2005. Socioeconomic status and mental illness: Tests of the social causation and selection hypotheses. *American Journal of Orthopsychiatry* 75 (1): 3–18.

Hughes, W. C. 2001. Schizophrenia is not contagious. *Psychiatric Services* 52 (3): 384.

Human Rights Watch. 2003. *Ill-Equipped: U.S. Prisons and Offenders with Mental Illness.* New York: Human Rights Watch.

James, D. L., and L. E. Glaze. 2006. *Mental Health Problems of Prison and Jail Inmates.* Washington, D.C.: U. S. Department of Justice, Bureau of Justice Statistics.

Janofsky, J. S., M. H. Dunn, E. J. Roskes, J. K. Briskin, and M. L. Rudolph. 1996. Insanity defense pleas in Baltimore city: An analysis of outcome. *American Journal of Psychiatry* 153 (11): 1464–68.

Janus, E. 1999. The use of social science and medicine in sex offender commitment. *New England Journal on Criminal and Civil Confinement* 23: 347–86.

Jennen, S. M. 1991. The IMD exclusion: A discriminatory denial of Medicaid funding for non-elderly adults in institutions for mental disorders. *William Mitchell Law Review* 17: 340–79.

Jessor, R., and S. L. Jessor. 1977. *Problem Behavior and Psychosocial Development: A Longitudinal Study of Youth*. New York: Academic Press.

John Jay College of Criminal Justice. 2004. *The Nature and Scope of Sexual Abuse of Minors by Catholic Priests and Deacons in the United States 1950–2002*. Washington, D.C.: U.S. Conference of Catholic Bishops.

Kelitz, I. and J. P. Fulton. 1984. *The Insanity Defense and Its Alternatives: A Guide for Policy Makers*. Williamsburg, Va.: Institute on Mental Disability and the Law, National Center for State Courts.

Kett, J. F. 1977. *Rites of Passage: Adolescence in America, 1790 to Present*. New York: Basic Books.

Kramer, M. 1977. Psychiatric services and the changing institutional scene: 1950–1985. DHEW Publication No. (ADM) 77–433. Washington, D.C.: U.S. Government Printing Office.

Kress, K. 2000. An argument for assisted outpatient treatment for persons with serious mental illness illustrated with reference to a proposed statute for Iowa. *Iowa Law Review* 85: 1269–1386.

Laing, R. D. 1960. *The Divided Self: An Existential Study in Sanity and Madness*. New York: Penguin.

Land, W. B., ed. 1995. *Psychopharmacological Options for Sex Offenders*. Kingston, N.Y.: Civic Research Institute.

Link, B. G., M. C. Lennon, and B. P. Dohrenwend. 1993. Socioeconomic status and depression: The role of occupations involving direction, control, and planning. *American Journal of Sociology* 98: 1351–87.

Liska, A. E., F. E. Markowitz, R. B. Whaley, and P. Bellair. 1999. Modeling the relationship between the criminal justice and mental health systems. *American Journal of Sociology* 104 (6): 174–75.

MacArthur Foundation Research Network on Adolescent Development and Juvenile Justice. 2003. Adjudicative competence to stand trial study: Summary of results. Available at http://www.mac-adoldev-juvjustice.org/page25.html.

Maines, D. R. 2000. The social construction of meaning. *Contemporary Sociology* 29 (4): 577–84.

Man guilty of killing five in racial shooting spree; may face death penalty. 2001. *Buffalo News*, May 10, p. A8.

Marques, J. K., M. Wiederanders, D. M. Day, C. Nelson, and A. van Ommeren. 2005. Effects of a relapse prevention program on sexual recidivism: Final results from California's sex offender treatment and evaluation project (SOTEP). *Sexual Abuse: Journal of Research and Treatment* 17 (1): 79–107.

Mechanic, D., and D. A. Rochefort. 1990. Deinstitutionalization: An appraisal of reform. *Annual Review of Sociology* 16: 301–27.

Melton, G. B., J. Petrila, N. G. Poythress, and C. Slobogin. 1997. *Competency to Stand Trial, Psychological Evaluations for the Courts: a Handbook for Mental Health Professionals and Lawyers*. New York: Guilford Press.

Milin, R., J. Greenstein, M. Johnson, and R. Friedman. 1991. The prevalence of abuse and co-existing DSM-III psychiatric disorders was evaluated in 111 juvenile offenders. *Journal of the American Academy of Child and Adolescent Psychiatry* 30 (4): 569–74.

Moffit, T. 1993. Adolescent-limited and life course persistent antisocial behavior: A developmental taxonomy. *Psychological Review* 100 (4): 674–701.

Moore, M. E., and V. A. Hiday. 2006. Mental health court outcomes: A comparison of re-arrest and re-arrest severity between mental health court and traditional court participants. *Law and Human Behavior* 30 (6): 659–74.

Morris, G. H., A. M. Haroun, and D. Naimark. 2004. Health law in the criminal justice system symposium: Competence to stand trial on trial. *Houston Journal of Health Law and Policy* 4: 193–238.

Morse, S. J. 2007. The non-problem of free will in forensic psychiatry and psychology. *Behavioral Sciences and the Law* 25 (2): 203–20.

Mulvey, E., and J. La Rosa. 1986. Delinquency cessation and adolescent development. *American Journal of Orthopsychiatry* 56 (2): 212–27.

Mumola, C. J. 2005. *Suicide and Homicide in State Prisons and Local Jails*. Washington, D.C.: U.S. Department of Justice, Bureau of Justice Statistics.

National Alliance for the Mentally Ill. 1999. *Families on the Brink*. Washington, D.C.: National Alliance for the Mentally Ill.

———. 2003. *The Criminalization of People with Mental Illness*. Washington, D.C.: National Alliance for the Mentally Ill.

National Alliance for the Mentally Ill and Public Citizen's Health Research Group. 1992. *Criminalizing the Seriously Mentally Ill: The Abuse of Jails as Mental Hospitals*. Washington, D.C.: National Alliance for the Mentally Ill.

National GAINS Center, Center for Mental Health Services. 2006. *Survey of Mental Health Courts*. Washington, D.C.: U.S. Department of Health and Human Services.

Nestor, P. G., D. Daggett, and M. Price. 1999. Competence to stand trial: A neuropsychological inquiry. *Law and Human Behavior* 23 (4): 397–412.

Nicholson, R. A., and K. E. Kugler. 1991. Competent and incompetent criminal defendants: A quantitative review of comparative research. *Psychological Bulletin* 109 (3): 355–70.

Nolan, J. L. 2003. Community courts and community justice: Commentary: redefining criminal courts: Problem-solving and the meaning of justice. *American Criminal Law Review* 40: 1541–65.

Office of Juvenile Justice and Delinquency Prevention. 2004. *Juvenile Suicide in Confinement: A National Survey.* Washington, D.C.: Office of Juvenile Justice and Delinquency Prevention.

Oppenheim, N. 1898. *The Development of the Child.* New York: Macmillan.

Otto, R., J. Greenstein, M. Johnson, R. Freidman, and J. Cocozza, eds. 1992. Prevalence of mental disorders among youth in the juvenile justice system. In J. J. Cocozza, ed., *Responding to the Mental Health Needs of Youth in the Juvenile Justice System.* Seattle: National Coalition for the Mentally Ill in the Criminal Justice System.

Ozarin, L. D., and S. S. Sharfstein. 1978. The aftermaths of deinstitutionalization: Problems and solutions. *Psychiatric Quarterly* 50 (2): 128–32.

Palermo, G. P., and M. A. Farkas. 2001. *The Dilemma of the Sexual Offender.* Springfield, Ill.: Charles C. Thomas.

Pasewark, R. A., and H. McGinley. 1986. Insanity plea: National survey of frequency and success. *Journal of Psychiatry and Law* 13: 101–8.

Patrick, C. J. 2006. *Handbook of Psychopathy.* New York: Guilford Press.

Pendleton, L. 1980. Treatment of persons found incompetent to stand trial. *American Journal of Psychiatry* 137 (9): 1098–1100.

Perinbanayagam, R. S. 1986. The meaning of uncertainty and the uncertainty of meaning. *Symbolic Interaction* 9: 105–26.

Perlin, M. L. 1994. *The Jurisprudence of the Insanity Defense.* Durham, N.C.: Carolina Academic Press.

———. 2000. *The Hidden Prejudice: Mental Disability on Trial.* Washington, D.C.: American Psychological Association.

Poythress, N. G., R. J. Bonnie, J. Monahan, and R. Otto. 2002. *Adjudicative Competency: The Macarthur Studies.* New York: Plenum Publishing.

Prentky, R. A. 1997. Arousal reduction in sexual offenders: A review of antiandrogen interventions. *Sexual Abuse: Journal of Research and Treatment* 9 (4): 335–47.

Prentky, R. A., A. F. Lee, R. A. Knight, and D. Cerce. 1997. Recidivism rates among child molesters and rapists: A methodological analysis. *Law and Human Behavior* 21 (6): 635–59.

Pustilnik, A. C. 2005. Prisons of the mind: Social value and economic inefficiency in the criminal justice response to mental illness. *Journal of Criminal Law and Criminology* 96: 217–65.

Radelet, M. L., S. D. Westerveldt, H. A. Humphrey, and J. A. Humphrey. 2001. *Wrongly Convicted: Perspectives on Failed Justice.* New Brunswick, N.J.: Rutgers University Press.

Ray, I. 1838/1983. *A Treatise on the Medical Jurisprudence of Insanity.* New York: DaCapo Press.

Redlich, A. D. 2004. Law and psychiatry: Mental illness, police interrogations, and the potential for false confessions. *Psychiatric Services* 55: 19–21.

Redlich, A. D., H. J. Steadman, J. R. Monahan, P. Clark, and J. Petrila. 2006. Patterns of practice in mental health courts: A national survey. *Law and Human Behavior* 30 (3): 347–62.

Reich, R., and L. Siegal. 1973. Psychiatry under siege: The chronically mentally ill shuffle to oblivion. *Psychiatric Annals* 3 (November): 3–5.

Ritsher, J., Warner, E. B., Johnson, J. G. and B. P. Dohrenwend. 2001. Inter-generational longitudinal study of social class and depression: A test of social causation and social selection models. *British Journal of Psychiatry* 178: s84–s90.

Roesch, R., P. A. Zapf, S. L. Golding, and J. L. Skeem. 1999. Defining and assessing competence to stand trial. In A. K. Hess and I. B. Weiner, eds., *The Handbook of Forensic Psychology*, 2nd ed., 327–50. New York: Wiley.

Rogers, R., N. Tillbrook, E. Chad, M. J. Vitacco, and K. W. Sewell. 2001. Recent interview-based measures of competency to stand trial: A critical review augmented with research data. *Behavioral Sciences and the Law* 19 (4): 503–18.

Rose, S. M. 1979. Deciphering deinstitutionalization: Complexities in policy and program analysis. *Milbank Memorial Fund Quarterly/Health and Society* 57 (4): 429–60.

Rothman, D. L. 1971. *The Discovery of the Asylum: Social Order and Disorder in the New Republic.* New York: Little, Brown.

Rousseau, G., M. Gill, D. Haycock, and M. Herwig. 2003. *Framing and Imagining Disease in Cultural History.* New York: Palgrave Macmillan.

Ryerson, E. 1978. *The Best-Laid Plans: America's Juvenile Court Experiment.* New York: Hill and Wang.

Sabshin, M. 1990. Turning points in twentieth-century American psychiatry. *American Journal of Psychiatry* 147 (10): 1267–74.

Sanders, W. B., ed. 1970. *Juvenile Offenders for a Thousand Years: Selected Readings from Anglo-Saxon Times to 1900.* Chapel Hill: University of North Carolina Press.

Sareyan, S. 1994. *The Turning Point: How Men of Conscience Brought about Major Change in the Care of America's Mentally Ill.* Washington, D.C.: American Psychiatric Press.

Scheck, B., P. Neufeld, and J. Dwyer. 2001. *Actual Innocence: When Justice Goes Wrong and How to Make It Right.* New York: Signet.

Scheid-Cook, T. 1991. Outpatient commitment as both social control and least-restrictive alternative. *Sociological Quarterly* 32 (1): 43–60.

Schopp, R. F. 2001. *Competence, Condemnation, and Commitment: An Integrated Theory of Mental Health Law.* Washington, D.C.: American Psychological Association.

Schulhofer, S. J. 1996. Two systems of social protection: Comments on the civil criminal distinction with particular reference to sexually violent predator laws. *Journal of Contemporary Legal Issues* 7: 69–98.

Scott, E. S., and T. Grisso. 1997. The evolution of adolescence: A developmental perspective on juvenile justice reform. *Journal of Criminal Law and Criminology* 88 (1): 137–89.

———. 2005. Developmental incompetence, due process, and juvenile justice policy. *North Carolina Law Review* 83: 793–845.

Scott, E. S., and L. Steinberg. 2003. Blaming youth. *Texas Law Review* 81 (3): 799–840.

Sentencing Project. 2002. *Mentally Ill Offenders in the Criminal Justice System: An Analysis and Prescription.* Washington, D.C.: Sentencing Project.

Siegel, L. A. 1996. Report of Lawrence A. Siegel, M.D., regarding Ralph Tortorici, January 7, 1996. Available at http://www.pbs.org/wgbh/pages/frontline/shows/crime/ralph/siegel.html.

Simon, R. J., and D. E. Aaronson. 1988. *The Insanity Defense: A Critical Assessment of Law and Policy in the Post-Hinckley Era.* New York: Praeger.

Simon, R., and H. Ahn-Redding. 2006. *The Insanity Defense, the World Over.* Lanham, Md.: Lexington Press.

Slate, R. N. 2003. From the jailhouse to Capitol Hill: Impacting mental health court legislation and defining what constitutes a mental health court. *Crime and Delinquency* 49 (1): 6–19.

Slobogin, C. 1994. Involuntary community treatment of people who are violent and mentally ill: A legal analysis. *Hospital and Community Psychiatry* 45 (7): 685–89.

Spector, M. and J. I. Kitsuse. 1977. *Constructing Social Problems.* Menlo Park, Calif.: Cummings.

Srole, L., T. S. Langner, S. T. Michael, P. Kirkpatrick, M. Opler, and T. A. C. Rennie. 1977. *Mental Health in the Metropolis: The Midtown Manhattan Study.* New York: Harper and Row.

Steadman, H. J., M. A. McGreevy, J. P. Morrissey, L. A. Callahan, P. C. Robbins, and C. Cirincione. 1993. *Before and After Hinckley: Evaluating Insanity Defense Reform.* New York: Guilford Press.

Steadman, H. J., J. Monahan, B. Duffee, E. Hartstone, and P. C. Robbins. 1984. The impact of state mental hospital deinstitutionalization on United States prison populations, 1968–1978. *Journal of Criminal Law and Criminology* 75 (2): 474–90.

Steadman, H. J., A. D. Redlich, P. Griffin, J. Petrila, and J. Monahan. 2005. From the referral to disposition: Case processing in seven mental health courts. *Behavioral Sciences and the Law* 23 (2): 215–26.

Steinberg, L. 2005. *Adolescence.* New York: McGraw-Hill.

Steinberg, L., and E. Cauffman. 1996. Maturity of judgment in adolescence: Psychosocial factors in adolescent decision-making. *Law and Human Behavior* 20 (3): 249–72.

Swedlow, K. 2003. Forced medication of legally incompetent prisoners: A primer. American Bar Association, Individual Rights and

Responsibilities; available at http://www.abanet.org/irr/hr/spring03/forcedmedication.html (accessed January 12, 2007).

Szasz, T. 1961. *The Myth of Mental Illness: A History of Involuntary Mental Hospitalization.* New York: Harper and Row.

Teplin, L. A. 1984. Criminalizing mental disorder: The comparative arrest rate of the mentally ill. *American Psychologist* 39: 794–813.

———. 1990. The prevalence of severe mental disorders among male urban jail detainees. *American Journal of Public Health* 80: 663–69.

Teplin, L., K. Abram, G. McClelland, M. Dulcan, and A. Mercle. 2002. Psychiatric disorders in youth juvenile detention. *Archives of General Psychiatry* 59 (12): 1133–43.

Thompson, M. 2005. *Race, Gender, and Mental Illness in the Criminal Justice System.* New York: LFB Scholarly Publishing.

Torrey, E. F. 1997. *Out of the Shadows: Confronting America's Mental Illness Crisis.* New York: John Wiley and Sons.

———. 2001. Outpatient commitment: What, why, and for whom. *Psychiatric Services* 52 (3): 337–41.

Torrey, E. F., J. Stieber, J. Ezekiel, S. M. Wolfe, J. Sharfstein, J. H. Noble, and L. M. Flynn. 1992. *Criminalizing the Seriously Mentally Ill.* Washington, D.C.: National Alliance for the Mentally Ill and Public Citizen Health Research Group.

U.S. Department of Justice. 2003. Civil Rights Division, Special Litigation Section. *Department of Justice Activities under the Civil Rights of Institutionalized Persons Act Fiscal Year 2003.* Washington, D.C.: U.S. Department of Justice.

———. 2004. *CRIPA Investigation of Adobe Mountain School and Black School in Phoenix, Arizona; and Catalina Mountain School in Tucson, Arizona, January 23, 2004.* Washington, D.C.: U.S. Department of Justice.

U.S. House of Representatives. 2004. Government Reform Committee. *Incarceration of Youth Who Are Waiting for Community Mental Health Services in the United States, July 2004.* Washington, D.C.: U.S. Congress.

Virginia Policy Design Team. 1994. *Mental Health Needs of Youth in Virginia's Juvenile Detention Centers.* Richmond: Virginia Policy Team.

Walker, L. 2006. Violence and exploitation against women and girls. *Annals of the New York Academy of Science* 1087: 142–57.

Walker, N. 1968. *Crime and Insanity in England,* vol. 1, *The Historical Perspective.* Chicago: Aldine Publishing Company.

Whitman, J. Q. 2003. *Harsh Justice: Criminal Punishment and the Widening Divide between America and Europe.* Oxford: Oxford University Press.

Winick, B. J., and J. Q. LaFond. 2003. *Protecting Society from Sexually Dangerous Offenders: Law, Justice, and Therapy.* Washington, D.C.: American Psychological Association.

Wollert, R. 2006. Low base rates limit expert certainty when current actuarials are used to identify sexually violent predators: An application of Bayes's theorem. *Psychology, Public Policy, and Law* 12 (1): 56–85.

Zanni, G., and L. de Veau. 1986. Inpatient stays before and after outpatient treatment. *Hospital and Community Psychiatry* 37 (9): 941–42.

Zapf, P. A., and J. L. Viljoen. 2003. Issues and considerations regarding the use of assessment instruments in the evaluation of competency to stand trial. *Behavioral Science and the Law* 21 (3): 351–67.

Zgoba, K. M., and L. M. Simon. 2005. Recidivism rates of sexual offenders up to seven years later: Does treatment matter? *Criminal Justice Review* 30 (2): 155–73.

Zimring, F. E. 1978. *Confronting Youth Crime: Report of the Twentieth Century Fund Task Force on Sentencing Policy toward Young Offenders.* New York: Holmes and Meier.

―――. 1998. *American Youth Violence.* New York: Oxford University Press.

Zonata, H. V. 2003. Competency to be executed and forced medication: *Singleton v. Norris. Journal of the American Academy of Psychiatry and the Law* 31: 372–76.

CASES

Addington v. Texas, 441 U.S. 418 (1979).

Ake v. Oklahoma, 470 U.S. 68 (1985).

Allen v. Illinois, 478 U.S. 364 (1986).

A.M. v. Luzerne County Juvenile Detention Center, 372 F. 3d 572 (3d Cir. 2004).

Board of County Commissioners v. Whitson, 132 P. 3d 920 (Kan. 2006).

Clark v. Arizona, 548 U.S. 735 (2006).

Davis v. United States, 165 U.S. 373 (1897).

Drope v. Missouri, 420 U.S. 162 (1975).

Durham v. United States, 214 F.2d 862 (1954).

Dusky v. United States, 362 U.S. 402 (1960).

Ford v. Wainwright, 477 U.S. 399 (1986).

Godinez v. Moran, 509 U.S. 389 (1993).

Heller v. Doe, 509 U.S. 312 (1993).

In re Care & Treatment of Hendricks, 912 P.2d 129 (Kan. 1996).

In re Gault, 387 U.S. 1 (1967).

In re Winship, 397 U.S. 358 (1970).

Kansas v. Crane, 534 U.S. 407 (2002).

Kansas v. Hendricks, 521 U.S. 346 (1997).

Lessard v. Schmidt, 349 F. Supp. 1078 (E.D. Wis. 1972).

Minnesota ex rel. Pearson v. Probate Court of Ramsey County, 309 U.S. 270 (1940).

M'Naghten's Case, 10 Clark and Finnelly 200 (1843).

O'Connor v. Donaldson, 422 U.S. 563 (1975).

Oregon v. Kinkel, 56 P. 3d 463 (Ore. Ct. App. 2002).

Panetti v. Dretke, 401 F. Supp. 2d 702 (W.D. Tex. 2004)

Panetti v. Dretke, 448 F.3d 815 (5th Cir. 2006)

Panetti v. Quarterman, 551 U.S. ———; 127 S. Ct. 2842 (2007).

Parsons v. Alabama, 2 So. 854 (1887).

Pate v. Robinson, 383 U. S. 375 (1966).

People v. Goldstein, 843 N.E. 2d 727 (N.Y. 2005).

People v. Tortorici, 709 N.E. 2d 87 (N.Y. 1999).

People v. Tortorici, 249 A.D. 2d 588 (App. Div. 1998).

Rex v. Arnold, 16 How. St. Tr. 695 (1724).

Rex v. Hadfield, 27 How. St. Tr. 1286 (1800).

Riggins v. Nevada, 504 U.S. 127 (1992).

Schriro v. Landrigan, 551 U.S., ———; 127 S. Ct. 1933 (2007).

Seling v. Young, 531 U.S. 250 (2001).

Sell v. United States, 539 U.S. 166 (2003).

Singleton v. Norris, 319 F. 3d 1018 (8th Cir. 2003).

Smith v. Commonwealth, 1 Duvall 226 (Ky. 1864).

Tate v. Florida, 864 So. 2d 44 (Fla. Dist. Ct. App. 2003)

United States v. Brawner, 471 F.2d 969 (1972).

Washington v. Harper, 494 U.S. 210 (1990).

Yates v. Texas, 171 S. W. 3d 215 (Tex. Crim. App. 2005).

STATUTES

Assisted Outpatient Treatment, N.Y. Ment. Hyg. L. § 960 (2007).

Civil Rights of Institutionalized Persons Act, 42 U.S.C. § 1997–1997j (2006).

Community Mental Health Centers Act of 1963, Pub. L. No. 88–164, 77 Stat. 282, 290–94 (1963).

Insanity, Texas Pen. Code § 8.01 (2006).

Insanity Defense, 18 U. S. C. § 17 (2006).

Insanity Test, Ariz. Rev. Stat. § 13–502(A) (2006).

Megan's Law, Pub. L. No. 104–145, 110 Stat. 1345 (1996).

Mental Disease or Defect Excluding Fitness to Proceed, N.Y. Crim. Proc. L. § 730 (1997).

National Law Enforcement and Mental Health Act of 2000, Pub. L. No. 106–515, 114 Stat. 2399 (2000).

Opinion on Ultimate Issue, Fed. R. Evid. 704(b) (2006).

Sexually Violent Predator Act of 1994, Kan. Stat., §§ 59–29a01 to 59–29a17 (1994 & Supp. 1997).

Supplemental Security Income for the Aged, Blind and Disabled, 42 U. S. C. §§1381–1385f (1972).

Social Security Act, 42 U.S. C. § 1396d (a) (1994).

Washington Community Protection Act, § 71.09.060 (3) (2007).

Index

About the Authors

PATRICIA E. ERICKSON is a professor of sociology and criminal justice at Canisius College, where she serves as chair of the department of sociology, anthropology, and criminal justice.

STEVEN K. ERICKSON is a forensic psychologist, practicing attorney, and a Mental Illness Research, Education, and Clinical Centers (MIRECC) fellow at Yale University.